Water Treatment and Sanitation

A handbook of simple methods for rural areas in developing countries

H.T. MANN
D. WILLIAMSON

PRACTICAL ACTION
Publishing

Practical Action Publishing Ltd
Schumacher Centre
Bourton on Dunsmore, Rugby,
Warwickshire CV23 9QZ, UK
www.practicalactionpublishing.org

First printed June 1973
First revised edition January 1976
Second revised edition July 1979
Third revised edition August 1982
Reprinted 1993
Transferred to digital printing 2013

ISBN 978-0-903031-23-3 Paperback

A catalogue record for this book is available from the British Library.

Since 1974, Practical Action Publishing (formerly Intermediate Technology
Publications and ITDG Publishing) has published and disseminated books
and information in support of international development work throughout
the world. Practical Action Publishing Ltd (Company Reg. No. 1159018)
is the wholly owned publishing company of Practical Action Ltd.
Practical Action Publishing trades only in support of its parent charity
objectives and any profits are covenanted back to Practical Action
(Charity Reg. No. 247257, Group VAT Registration No. 880 9924 76).

Contents

	Preface	3
	Introduction	4
1	The Selection of a Water Source and Simple Water Testing	6
2	Water Supply	14
3	Water Treatment	38
4	Foul Water and Excreta Disposal	51
5	Sewage Treatment	60
6	Final Water and Sludge Disposal	70
7	Temporary and Emergency Treatment	81
	Appendix	88
	Glossary	92
	Further Reading	95

Preface

With the publication of this second edition of *Water Treatment and Sanitation* the Intermediate Technology Development Group takes a further step in the implementation of its primary purpose – that is, to fill the 'knowledge gap' which still exists from the point of view of poor communities and their helpers, who must resort to simple and cheap methods to fulfil their basic needs.

Few needs are more basic than those of good water and proper sanitation. The importance of these facilities to health needs no emphasis; equally great is their importance to the development of self-respect and the spirit of self-reliance.

When it comes to water supplies and waste disposal, the rural areas of most developing countries show widespread neglect. To a large extent this is due to the firmly established view that the cost of these facilities, heavy even in areas of high population density, is completely out of reach in extended rural situations. The possibility of applying low-cost techniques is often unknown. It is the purpose of this handbook to make the possibilities of applying low-cost techniques more widely known.

If those who have designed, built, or operated any of the devices described, or any other simple systems, will be good enough to send information of their field experience to one or all of the organisations listed on the last page, it may be possible, before long, to build up a much fuller body of field-tested knowledge than is now being presented.

It is the special concern and hope of the Intermediate Technology Development Group to help in the establishment of an efficient international communications system, by which the knowledge of proven methods and techniques, appropriate to the economic potential of poor communities, can flow fully and freely to those who need it most.

Finally I should like to express our gratititude to the authors who have put so much work into the original and revised editions of this handbook, and to the Director of the Water Pollution Research Station, Stevenage, Herts, where much of the drafting was carried out. H.T. Mann, a member of the staff of this research station, has had wide experience overseas in tropical countries and D. Williamson, at present with a water authority in England, has previously served with Consulting Engineers in developing countries.

E.F. Schumacher

Introduction

An adequate supply of good quality safe water is essential to the promotion of public health. In many less developed parts of the world, particularly in tropical areas, the health hazards caused by polluted water supplies are more numerous and more serious than those in temperate and more developed areas.

The purpose of this handbook is to put together in a simple and logical form various aspects which must be considered when investigating the development of a water supply and sewage disposal scheme for a small community. This could be a rural village or small town, or a school or hospital situated too far from a piped system of water supply and therefore requiring its own source, treatment and pipelines, and sewage disposal.

It is based partly on reports submitted by one of the authors, during a research project on small water supplies and sanitation in Uganda, partially financed by the Ministry of Overseas Development, and partly on experience gained by the authors on water supply projects both in England and overseas.

This booklet is not intended as a text book for engineers, although they may find some sections useful for rapid reference, but it is intended for technicians, leaders of rural communities, administrators of schools or hospitals and others who wish to develop a water supply and sewage disposal scheme for their own use. It is hoped that each section will give some help in solving the many problems involved in such an exercise.

The sections giving formulae and their use may also help in the documentation of information required by a central authority when considering the development and financing of a supply.

The drawings showing simple apparatus could be copied and used by a local craftsman to improve the quality of a supply.

It is important when considering a water supply, to consider at the same time the disposal of the waste water after use. It is easy to introduce a cycle in which the waste water from the community pollutes the supply. This must be considered when investigating sources, and if necessary access to the land surrounding a source must be restricted. This will be considered further in the section dealing with the choice of a source.

The characteristics of water available vary widely both chemically and biologically, so that no single system of water treatment can be universally applicable. All

4

water sources must be considered on their individual merits. Referring to the table of contents it will be seen the handbook is divided into chapters covering the basic steps from water sources to effluent disposal.

Many of the methods of water and sewage treatment described in this handbook are based on the standard practices used in developed countries. They are, however, adapted to suit rural tropical conditions, and much material has been included which has been derived from experience in tropical areas drawn from a variety of sources, and is not normally found in standard temperate-zone practice.

Chapters 1 to 6 describe methods which may be applied in sequence, from the selection of a water source, the transport of water, the treatment of water, the disposal of wastes, sewage treatment and the final disposal of treated wastes, and the by-products of treatment processes. In each chapter a number of alternatives is described, some suitable for self-help situations, others which may be more suitable for larger communities. In building a complete system the subjects of the six chapter headings should be considered in sequence and methods suited to the individual circumstances may be selected. Clearly the same plan of action need not be followed in every situation, but the potential development of a situation with consequent changes in requirements for water supply and sanitation should not be overlooked.

A glossary will be found at the end of the book which explains the meaning of technical terms used in the text. Some useful factors, formulae, metric conversions and abbreviations are given at the end of Chapter 2.

Where specialist advice is needed the Public Health Authorities in most countries are able to provide this either directly or by referring to some other government department. When specialist advice is sought it is important that information supplied should be as accurate and reliable as possible.

Conditions in developing countries vary a great deal and there is a continuing need for the proper evaluation of water treatment and sewage treatment systems especially those of a temporary nature and those which include novel or experimental devices. Publication of such information both locally and in the technical and professionals journals is of considerable importance in advancing development.

Chapter One

The Selection of a Water Source and Simple Water Testing

The effectiveness of any source will, in the first instance, depend on the local rainfall, its pattern throughout the year, the evaporation and natural storage available. Most of this information will be available locally. The following summary of typical sources is based on those available in Uganda, but is generally applicable in any tropical country.

1. Rivers and Streams

In the tropics these waters are almost invariably soft, containing relatively low concentrations of dissolved salts, although this does not necessarily apply elsewhere. They are often affected by faecal pollution, usually greatest in small streams near settlements. The quality of the water can vary considerably with rainfall, but turbidity can be expected at most times. Slow flowing rivers can contain considerable amounts of organic colouring matter.

2. Lakes

Large lakes form obvious ample reservoirs of water. In general the water quality is fairly good and consistent but may well be polluted, and in particular contain bilharzia contamination, near the shores. Near areas of industrial and agricultural development, and sewage and industrial effluent discharges, there is an increasing danger of algal growth forming which may effect the water to such an extent that it is impracticable to consider it as a source for public water supply.

3. Swamp waters

Swamp waters, which can include slowly flowing rivers, generally contain faecal pollution and other organic material in comparatively high concentrations, giving rise to an unacceptable colour. These waters are usually acidic.

4. Springs and boreholes

In areas of impervious substrate, springs and boreholes can give a reliable supply and if properly maintained, and sufficiently distant from pit privies and soakpits, a supply free, or almost free from faecal pollution.

Springs and boreholes have been considered together as both derive their supply from underground. In the case of springs the water is naturally discharged from the ground where its flow is impeded by a less permeable strata. It is essential that careful control is maintained of the land near the seat of the spring in order to prevent pollution. Quite often a source like this can be utilized to provide a supply to a community, without pumping, at minimum cost and maintenance (Fig. 1).

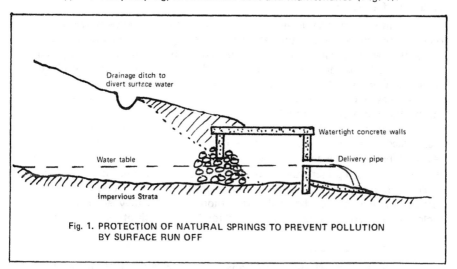

Fig. 1. PROTECTION OF NATURAL SPRINGS TO PREVENT POLLUTION BY SURFACE RUN OFF

A well or borehole must be dug or sunk into the permeable strata and the water lifted manually or by mechanical pumps. Again it is essential that careful control is kept on the land adjacent to the well head. It is usually advisable to prevent surface water entering the well by sealing the top section with brick or concrete. In many areas, underground water may contain iron in solution or suspension, requiring treatment as discussed in the appropriate section of this handbook.

Alongside major rivers there are often large gravel deposits which retain water even when the river may seasonally dry up. The water drawn from boreholes in such river gravels will usually be of a considerably better bacteriological quality than the river water itself. Wells in river gravel need to be lined with perforated steel tubes to hold back the gravel. The size of the perforations will to some extent depend on the particle size of the gravel and its sand and silt content, but 10 mm slots 150 mm long situated in groups of four every half metre may well suffice. Shaftdriven borehole pumps or submersible pumps described in the section on pumping will then be required.

5. Rainwater catchments

Rainfall can be collected as run-off, from impervious areas such as corrugated iron roofs or artifically formed catchments of concrete or other watertight material. The size of storage tank required depends entirely on the rainfall and its distribution throughout the year. The storage tank must be of sufficient size to give the daily demand over the maximum expected drought period. The catchment area must then be of sufficient size to guarantee that the tank will fill again before the next dry spell.

Selection of a source

Where more than one possible source is available the choice should be made in order of priorities: firstly, the reliability of the source, secondly, its purity and lastly, the ease with which it can be supplied to the consumers. If a large supply is being planned from an unexploited source, the services of an analytical laboratory should be employed to assess the quality and advise on necessary treatment. Small communities may not be able to call upon these services but the assessment of purity should not be left entirely to judgement.

Natural bodies of water of most kinds are not uniform, they vary in composition from place to place, from time to time in the course of a day, and from season to season. When taking water samples for examination, care should be taken to ensure that the samples represent the body of water as much as possible. Multiple samples taken over a period of time will provide much more information than a single sample. Samples should be analysed without delay as they are liable to certain biological and chemical changes if kept for long periods at normal temperatures.

Simple tests for water quality

The analysis of water and effluents is a job for a skilled laboratory worker and cannot be fully covered in this handbook. There are however some simple tests which can be carried out with a minimum of skill which can be of value when the choice must be made between different sources of water, and subsequently if a treatment plant is installed it is useful to be able to check the performance of the plant from time to time. Where chlorination is employed regular tests must be made for residual chlorine.

Taking samples for testing or analysis

A clean glass or plastic bottle sealed with a rubber or plastic stopper must be used. If the vessel has been previously used as a container, it must be carefully inspected to ensure that no trace of the previous contents remains on container or stopper. It any smell can be detected, it should be rejected, or cleaned until no smell remains. The bottle should then be washed out 3 times with a small quantity of the water to be sampled, and then filled and labelled immediately with time, date and place. If the sample is drawn from a stream or other body of open water, the bottle should be plunged in at a point a short distance from the bank and care taken not to allow gross floating debris or any mud disturbed from the bottom to enter the bottle. Samples taken in this way are suitable for laboratory analysis but not for bacteriological tests. Such samples should be not less than 2 litres (½ gal) and should be sent for analysis without delay. Much useful information can be obtained by observing a sample drawn in a glass cylinder. Turbidity can be noted and may be measured by comparison with other samples or with prepared standards. The usefulness of quiescent settlement can be observed and also the nature of suspended matter, whether animal, vegetable, or mineral, can be estimated. Bilharzia cercaria and some other parasites can be visually identified. Precipation of iron compounds can sometimes be observed.

Test 1. Chlorine demand – for waters to be treated

Required

a. A clean glass vessel 500 ml capacity or more.
b. Stock chlorine solution containing 1 per cent available chlorine.
c. Dropping pipette calibrated to deliver 20 drops per ml.
d. Means to measure residual chlorine.

The stock chlorine solution can be prepared from dry chloride of lime (35 per cent available chlorine) or HTH (High Test Hypochlorite 70 per cent available chlorine) dissolved in clean water. This solution should be kept in a dark bottle with a glass stopper but as it does not keep well it should be checked from time to time with the residual chlorine test after appropriate dilution.

Test procedure – measure 500 ml of sample into a clean glass vessel and add 3 drops (0.15ml) of stock chlorine solution. Mix and allow to stand for 30 minutes in a shady place to enable the chlorine to react with the impurities in the water, then find the residual chlorine by any method available (three methods are described below). The initial chlorine dose given by 3 drops of 1 per cent solution in 500 ml of water is 3 mg/l. If the residual chlorine is subtracted from the initial chlorine value the chlorine demand is obtained.

Example: Chlorine dose 3 drops to
500 ml = 3 mg Cl_2/1

Residual chlorine found after
30 mins = 1 mg Cl_2/l

Chlorine demand = 3−1=2 mg/l Cl_2

If the sample is heavily polluted the initial chlorine dose of 3 mg/l may be insufficient to leave any residual chlorine. In this case repeat the test with a higher chlorine dose. The higher the chlorine demand the greater the pollution present.

Test 2. Residual chlorine concentration – for chlorinated waters and for use in Test 1. Three methods can be employed for this test. The first requires no special equipment, the others are more sensitive but require an instrument called the BDH (British Drug Houses) Lovibond Comparator. These tests should be carried out immediately the samples are available. No delay is possible.

Method A – BDH Chlorotex method

9

Required — BDH Chlorotex reagent, this is supplied with a colour matching card.

Test procedure — Take 50 ml of sample in a clean glass vessel and add 5 ml of Chlorotex reagent. A colour develops immediately if chlorine is present.

		mg/l Cl_2
White milky fluorescence	—	nil
Faintly pink and milky	—	0.1
Pink	—	0.2
Red	—	0.5
Purple	—	0.6
Violet	—	0.8
Blue	—	1.0 or more

Method B — BDH Comparator and O-tolidine reagent.
Required — a. BDH comparator with 2 10 ml tubes.
b. Acid O-tolidine reagent — This may be obtained ready for use or it may be made by dissolving 1 gm AR. O-tolidine in 100 ml AR. hydrochloric acid and adding distilled water to make 1000 ml.
c. BDH comparator disc — There are three alternatives:

3/2A 0.1 to 1.0 mg/l chlorine
3/2AB 0.15 to 2.0 mg/l chlorine
KMA 0.05 to 0.5 mg/l chlorine and 6.0 to 7.6 pH.

Test procedure — Put 10 ml sample in each tube and place them in the comparator. Add 0.1 ml (2 drops) of reagent to the right hand tube, mix and allow to stand for 10 minutes. Compare the colours visible through the viewing windows against the sky, with the operator's back to the sun. Rotate the disc until the colours match. The residual chlorine figure may be read in the window in the lower right hand corner of the instrument.

Method C — BDH comparator with Palin's DPD reagent.
Required — a. BDH comparator with 2 10-ml tubes.
b. DPD chlorine tablets No. 4.
c. BDH comparator disc — There are two alternatives:
3/40/A 0.1 to 1.0 mg/l chlorine
3/40/B 0.2 to 4.0 mg/l chlorine
d. Special dulling screen provided with the disc which must be fitted to the right hand viewing window of the comparator.

Test Procedure — Put 10 ml sample in a tube and place it in the left compartment of the comparator. Place a reagent tablet in another tube and add about 1 cm depth of water and allow the tablet to dissolve. Add more sample until the tube contains 10 ml and place the tube in the right hand compartment. Compare after 2 minutes and read the chlorine figure in the lower right hand window.

Test 3. pH — on all waters — The pH of a water is a measure of its acidic activity, not of the acid concentration in it. This is of importance because small concentrations of strongly acidic substances have different chemical effects from larger concentrations of weakly acidic substances, especially with regard to chlorination and corrosion characteristics. Neutral waters are said to have a pH of 7.0, acid waters have a pH less than 7.0 and alkaline waters have a pH greater than 7.0. The desirable limits of pH for water supplies are between 6.8 and 7.6 though 6.5 to 8.2 is acceptable. If pH values of water supplies fall outside these limits then specialized advice should be sought. There are 2 suitable methods for finding the pH value.

Method A   Indicator method using BDH comparator.
Required —   BDH Comparator and 2 10-ml tubes
              BDH Indicator and disc of the necessary range, i.e.
   pH 5.2 — 6.8 Bromocresol purple disc 2/1 G
   pH 6.0 — 7.6 Bromo Thymol blue disc 2/1 H
   pH 6.8 — 8.4 Phenol red (requires dulling screen) disc 2/1 J
   pH 7.2 — 8.8 Cresol red disc 2/1 K
   pH 8.0 — 9.6 Thymol blue disc 2/1 L

Test Procedure — Put 10 ml sample in each tube and add 10 drops (0.5 ml) indicator to the right hand tube. Be sure that the disc is the correct disc and if the dulling screen is necessary that it is in place. Match the colours and read the pH value.

Method B — Indicator method using test papers.

There are many kinds of pH test papers which are used by dipping small pieces of the test paper into the sample and comparing the colour produced with the colour chart provided.

The Examination of Water in the Field

Although water analysis is usually thought of as a job for skilled laboratory workers there are many situations in the field where water is used without treatment by local people who wish to improve the quality of the water but have no access to laboratory services. Water that has been consumed by people for long periods without suffering obvious deterioration in health is unlikely to contain any acutely dangerous concentrations of harmful organisms or substances, though continuous consumption of low concentrations may have harmful effects in the long term, and there may be periods when harmful concentrations occur temporarily. The testing of such a supply may be usefully related to the treatment measures that may be available locally to improve the quality.

Water quality is mainly affected by five groups of substances:

1. Toxic substances

a) Arsenic, lead and other heavy metals, occasionally found in deep boreholes. Analysis is specific and trained chemists are necessary. If present in harmful concentrations the effects on the health of local people is usually obvious and contaminated boreholes should be sealed. Treatment of such waters is difficult and should not be attempted without expert control.

b) Toxic organic substances such as phenols, pesticides, etc. These are usually the result of pollution that is rarely found in rural areas. Otherwise should be considered as above.

c) Nitrates are toxic to small babies, and concentrations above about 10 mg/l as N (45 mg/l NO_3) should be regarded as suspect. With certain uncommon exceptions nitrates occur as an end product of the biodegradation of animal excreta such as might be found close to pit privies, manure heaps or yards containing livestock. All such areas should not be situated near water sources. Tests can be made but if these circumstances do not indicate a probable source and no evidence of methaemoglobinaemia is observed in small babies locally, they are probably not necessary. Nitrates are not easy to remove from water, avoidance of polluted situations is the best prevention.

2. High Concentrations of dissolved salts. If the local people are able to tolerate the raw water without harmful effects there is no urgent need to rectify this.

3. Suspended matter. This may not be injurious to health but is always better removed. The usual methods of simple treatment are settlement and filtration. Much useful information can therefore be obtained by settling a sample, say 1 litre in a tall clear glass bottle for a period of an hour or more. Observation will indicate how much improvement of clarity can be achieved by settlement in a given time. Observation of the solid particles may indicate sand or coarse mineral solids, vegetable particles, algae, protozoa, bilharzia cercaria and other forms of life. A magnifier is useful for this purpose. If a second sample is filtered through filter paper or clean blotting paper it will be a guide to the likely improvement possible with sand filters. If the filtrate is coloured it may indicate dissolved organic matter probably derived from swamps.

4. Acid and alkaline substances. Tests can be made with pH papers. Values below 6.5 indicate a corrosive water requiring treatment with limestone. Values above about 9.0 require treatment outside the scope of small rural projects and should be rejected if possible.

5. Organic matter derived from faecal pollution. May contain disease organisms. Specific bacteriological tests are not usually practicable but the general health of local people is a good indication of serious risks. In general most surface waters should be regarded as polluted and every effort made to filter and disinfect. Some borehole waters are found that are not polluted, thus may be preferable sources if available. The chlorine demand test is a useful measure of organic pollution and can be used for comparing different waters.

Other useful tests that can sometimes be carried out in the field are the tests for ammonia using Nesslers solution. Recent faecal pollution always contains ammonia and if it is found bacterial contamination is likely. As the pollution degrades, the ammonia concentration usually falls and the bacterial population also falls so that a degree of comparative assessment can be made on waters from different sources or waters before and after treatment processes. Another useful test is the test for oxygen absorbed in 30 minutes from acidified $KMnO_4$ (potassium permanganate), which gives a useful measure of organic impurity related to the organic carbon concentration, and can also be used for comparative purposes. Further advice can be obtained on these tests if required.

There are many other tests that can be employed but they are not within the scope of this handbook to describe. Wherever the assistance or advice of a trained chemist is available it should be used.

Chapter Two

Water Supply

Demand for water

An estimate of the probable demand for water by the community must first be made and compared with the yield of the source. The demand must first be considered on an hourly basis and then on a daily basis. Where storage of water is available such as a small reservoir, the average demand over a dry season must also be considered.

The pipeline from any holding tank (or from the source, if there is no holding tank) or reservoir, must be adequate to take the peak demand at any time of day. The peak rate may be five times the average rate. If there is no holding tank to balance out the varying demands throughout the day, then the source itself must be capable of yielding the peak demand. The advantage of having even a small reservoir or tank to give extra supplies at times of peak demand can easily be seen.

It is often difficult to estimate what the demand on a new source will be, but the following factors are given as a guide:-

1. Each tap will take about 11 litres (2½ gallons) per minute and in the case of a communal tap it may well run continuously for long spells. Precautions should be taken to ensure that taps are turned off after use.
2. Where water is carried by hand from taps to houses the demand will probably not exceed 18 litres (4 gallons) per person per day, but once the water is piped to each house this figure will rise quickly. With a single tap the quantity may go up to 45 litres (10 gallons) per head per day but with a fully piped system, with bathroom and toilet, the quantity will almost certainly exceed 225 litres (50 gallons) per person per day.
3. The demand where a community is living together, such as a school or hospital, will probably be less than the above estimates but can be estimated on similar lines.
4. The loss of water through faulty jointing of the pipelines and poor plumbing can easily be 25 per cent of the total demand. It is therefore essential, when either the source is limited or the water is pumped or treated, that extreme care is taken when the supply is installed to make certain that this loss is kept to a minimum.

Materials for pipelines

Materials generally available for water supply pipelines:-

1. Steel tube

Steel tube, either black or galvanized with screwed joints is widely available, in sizes from 10 to 150 mm (½ to 6 inches) diameter. Galvanized pipe is generally preferable as it resists to some extent internal and external corrosion.

2. Spun iron pipe

Spun iron pipe with either flanged or socket joints may be available in sizes from 75 to 150 mm (3 to 6 inches) diameter, or larger. These pipes are bitumen dipped and generally more resistant to corrosion than steel tube.

3. Asbestos cement pipes

These are available in sizes similar to spun, or cast iron, but are highly resistant to corrosion. They are to some extent brittle and need careful handling.

4. Rigid PVC pipe

Generally available from 50 to 150 mm (2 to 6 inches) diameter and above. They are light to handle, resistant to corrosion and easily laid, usually available in lengths up to 10 m which can easily be handled by one person. Joints are easily made and a wide variety of fittings is available.

5. Polythene pipes

Generally available from 10 to 75 mm (½ to 3 inches) diameter in long lengths, polythene tube is the ideal solution to all small-bore pipe runs. It is relatively cheap, easy to handle and lay and, being available in long lengths, less likely to have leaking joints. Polythene pipe can be supplied with a wide variety of fittings and can be coupled to other types of pipe. Polythene pipe is not completely resistant to attack by rodents and some tropical insects. Polythene pipe laid underground should be bedded in sand or soil with no sharp stones present; laid overground should be adequately supported to prevent sagging. Certain grades of polythene and PVC pipe contain traces of objectionable soluble substances; these should be avoided by ordering material that is known to be suitable for water supply.

Hydraulic considerations for the design of a water supply scheme

All water supply schemes involve the flow of water through pipes. This flow involves the consideration of the frictional resistance of the water against the pipe walls. Friction depends on the nature of the surface of the walls and the velocity of flow through the pipe. The energy lost in overcoming the frictional resistance is expressed as a loss of pressure head, usually measured in metres of water.

Consider the following simple example of flow in a pipeline from a reservoir (Fig. 2).

Under static conditions the pressure at point B will be H metres. As the velocity of flow in the pipeline increases, the pressure head at B will reduce to h metres where h = H − H_f being the head lost due to friction (Fig. 2).

$H_f = K \dfrac{LV^2}{d}$ where K is a constant dependent on the type and nature of pipe-line.

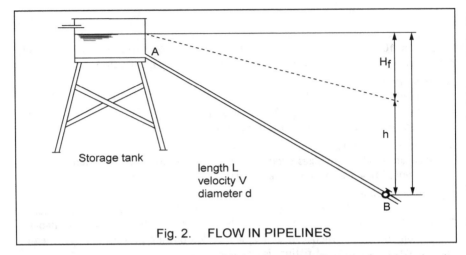

Fig. 2.   FLOW IN PIPELINES

Storage tank

length L
velocity V
diameter d

H_f

h

A

B

Charts have been prepared on the basis of this formula for high density polythene pipe and for rigid PVC pipe, or galvanised iron pipe, which give the head loss in metres per 1000 metres of pipe for different flows and different diameters of pipe (Figs. 3, 4, 5).

When estimating the flow through a pipeline to a community the maximum demand at any instant must be considered. A chart has been prepared giving an indication of how many taps in a group of taps may be running at once. For a small number of taps, all may run at once but as the number of taps increases all will not be required at the same time. This chart gives an indication of the peak demand that can be expected (Fig. 6).

The pressure required to drive the water throuqh the standpipe and tap must be considered and for design purposes 10 metres (30 ft) of head should be allowed if possible. An example of the use of these tables is shown in the following problem.

A village water supply system is to have 35 communal taps. From Fig. 6 it can be assumed that 15 taps will be used at once giving a peak demand of 165 litres per minute. The village is situated 4,000 metres from the reservoir which has a water level of 300 metres above sea level and the village is about 275 metres above sea level.

From the chart for rigid PVC pipe (Fig. 3) and using a 100 mm pipe, the 2.75 litres per second (165 litres per minute) vertical line is crossed by the 100 mm sloping line at a friction loss reading of 1.5 metres per 1,000 metres. So in the 4,000 metres of pipeline the pressure head loss due to friction will be 6 metres. So the pressure at the village at this flow will be (300 − 6) − 275, that is 19 metres, not 25 metres as would be available under static conditions.

Assuming that 10 metres head of water are required to pass a reasonable flow through the tap, then no tap in this village situated above (300 − 6) − 10 or 284 metres above sea level would receive a reasonable flow.

(continued on p.20)

16

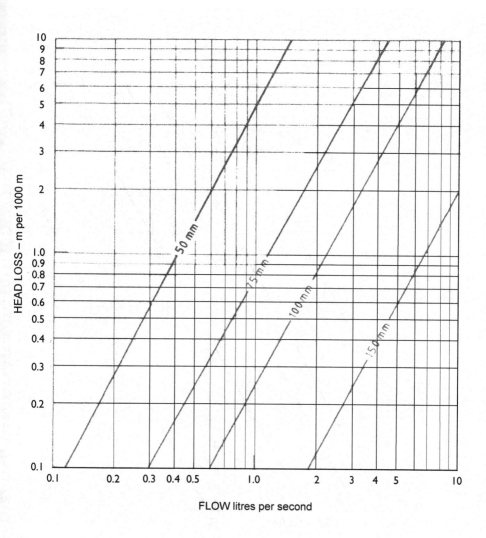

Fig. 3. HEAD LOSS IN PIPELINES
(Rigid PVC Class C)

17

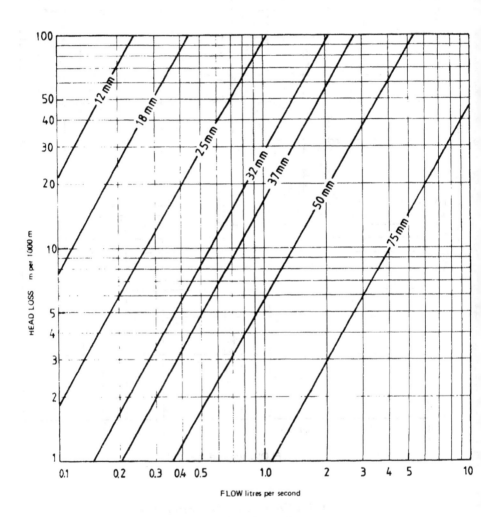

Fig. 4.   HEAD LOSS IN PIPELINES
(High density polythene pipe)

18

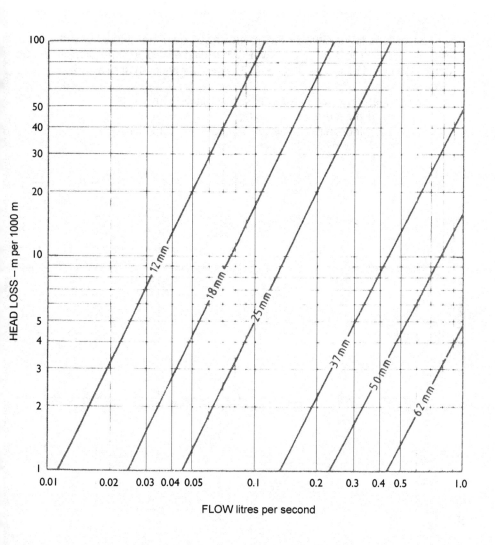

Fig. 5. HEAD LOSS IN PIPELINES
(Galvanised Steel)

19

Possibly one tap is situated 500 metres away from the village but at the same level of 275 metres above sea level. What diameter polythene pipe would be required to give 11 litres per minute (0.18 litres per second) at this tap?

From above: pressure head available in village 20m
pressure loss in the tap   10m
friction loss available in 500m   10m
of pipe (or 20m per 1000m)

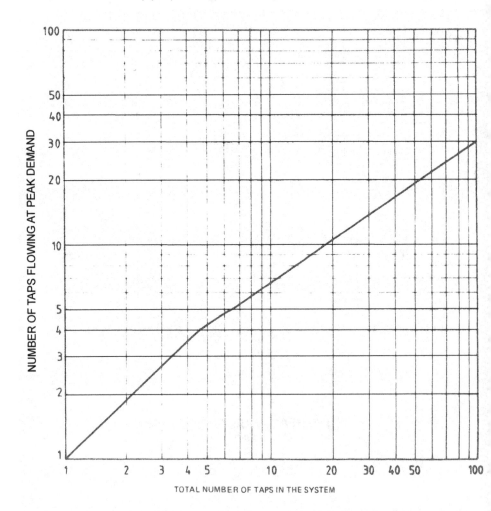

Fig. 6.   INSTANTANEOUS DEMAND IN A SMALL WATER SYSTEM

From the polythene pipe chart (Fig. 4) reading the loss of 20m per 1,000m horizontally and 0.18 litres per second vertically a 19mm (¾ inch) pipeline is indicated.

A larger size could be used and then if necessary, in the future, a further tap added. If for economy a 12mm (½ inch) diameter pipe were used, the maximum flow would be 6 litres (1.3 gallons) per minute.

A similar calculation of the frictional head loss is required when determining the capacity of a pump. Here is a further example of the use of the charts in connection with a pumping pipeline. The water level in a well is 20 metres below ground level. The top water level in the tank to which the water is pumped is 80 metres above the ground level at the well head, but situated 1500 metres away. It has been estimated that the community will use 22,500 litres (5000 gallons) per day and it has been decided to pump 12 hours per day. What horse-power pump will be required?

The pumping rate will be 30 litres per minute. The pumping head is made up as follows —

Lift from the well to ground level   — 20 m
Lift from ground level to reservoir   — 80 m
Frictional resistance along pipeline — H_f

Using the polythene pipe chart (Fig. 4) at 0.5 litres per second the following results are obtained:-

Pipe diameter		Friction head	Friction head in
Metric	Imperial	per 1000 m	pipeline 1500 m long
25 mm	1 inch	29 m	43.5 m
32 mm	1¼ inch	8.5 m	12.8 m
37 mm	1½ inch	4.7 m	7.0 m
50 mm	2 inch	1.8 m	2.7 m

The head loss with a 25 mm pipe is large compared with the total head to be pumped. Either a 32 mm or 37 mm pipe would be adequate. Take the 32 mm pipe:

Static head   100 m
Friction head   12.8 m
                    ——————
Total pumping head 112.8 m
                    ——————

From the formula given on page 37, the horse power required

$$= \frac{0.5 \times 112.8}{76} = 0.74 \text{ HP}$$

Assuming an overall efficiency of 35%, a 2 HP motor is required.

A chart has been prepared (Fig. 11) giving an indication of the power required in kilowatts for differing flows and total pumping heads as the unit efficiency increases with size.

Similar hydraulic considerations must be made when designing the diameter and fall on sewers where the flow is by gravity. Here the usual minimum diameter is 150 mm (6 inch) in order to avoid blockages. The sewer should be laid in straight lines and with a constant fall between manholes so that the line can be cleared with rods if necessary. Design chart Fig. 7 shows the flows at varying gradients, but the sewers should not be laid flatter than the line indicated, so that the velocity of flow is great enough to carry all solids along the sewer.

Measurement of yield of a source

Where the flow from a spring or small stream is limited, it is essential that the flow is measured regularly for at least one year in order to assess the yield. In most slow-flowing streams, weirs or V-notches can be used for flow measurement.

This can be done by putting a weir across the stream (Fig. 8) and making sure that all the water passes over the weir. A timber structure with a weir of a known length will suffice for most purposes but a block or concrete structure with a steel plate will give more accurate readings. If accurate readings at low flows are required, a 90^0 V-notch weir will give good results. The water level over the crest of the weir must be measured about 30 cm back from the crest where the flow is steady. These water levels can be converted directly to flows using the charts (Figs. 9 and 10). The estimate of yield of a borehole is more difficult and it may safely be said that the only practical way of ascertaining this is by pumping at different rates over periods of several days. The flow from the pump can be measured using weirs as already described.

Pumping plant

The choice between the use of mechanical or manual pumping plant will depend on the quantity of water required from the source, the availability of finance and the means of operating the plant either by electricity or a small petrol-driven engine.

Several types of pumping plant are briefly covered here.

Mechanical pumps

Any mechanical pump should be ordered from the supplier to pump a specified quantity of water against the total lift. The prime mover, or the pump drive, will either be an electric motor or small petrol engine, and should be ordered together with the pump.

Types of pumps

a. Horizontal or vertical direct-drive pumps.

Small pumps, electrically or engine driven, are now readily available at most

(Continued on p.28)

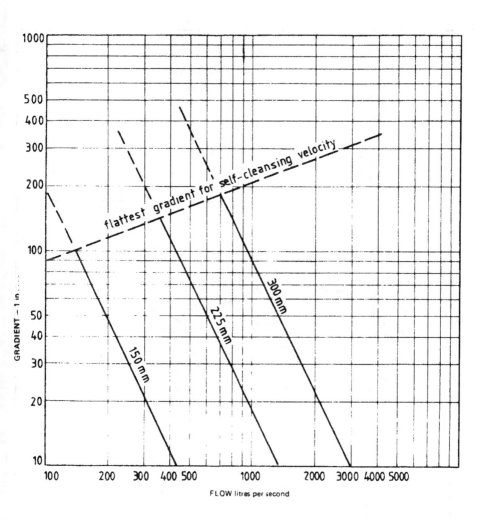

Fig. 7.   FLOW IN SEWERS AND DRAINS

23

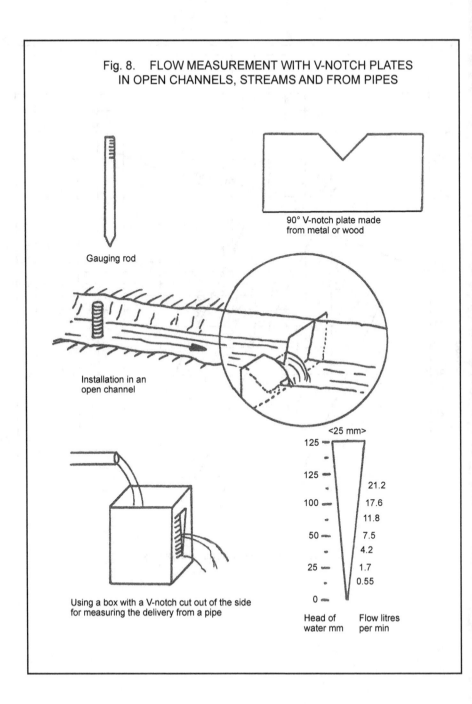

Fig. 8.   FLOW MEASUREMENT WITH V-NOTCH PLATES
IN OPEN CHANNELS, STREAMS AND FROM PIPES

90° V-notch plate made
from metal or wood

Gauging rod

Installation in an
open channel

Using a box with a V-notch cut out of the side
for measuring the delivery from a pipe

<25 mm>

Head of water mm	Flow litres per min
125	
125	
	21.2
100	17.6
	11.8
50	7.5
	4.2
25	1.7
	0.55
0	

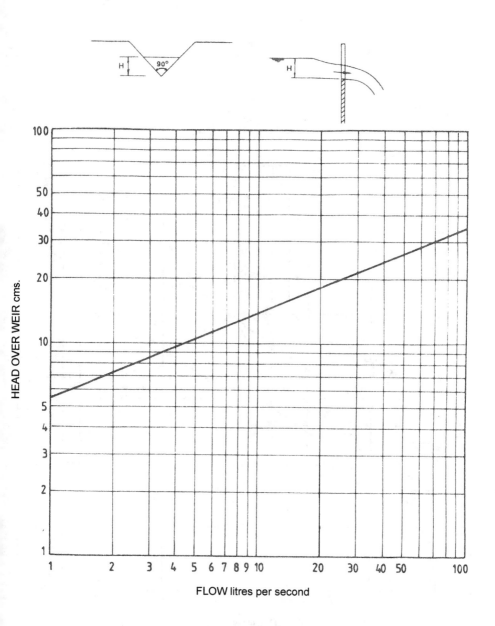

FLOW litres per second

Fig. 9.   FLOW MEASUREMENT WITH A 90° V-NOTCH WEIR

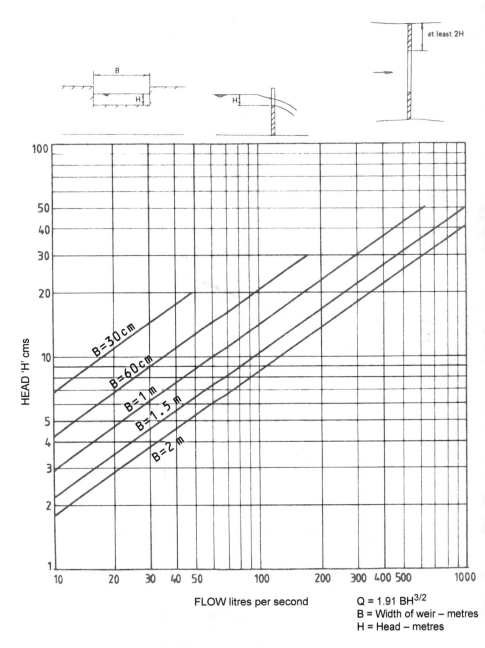

HEAD 'H' cms

FLOW litres per second

$$Q = 1.91 \, BH^{3/2}$$
B = Width of weir – metres
H = Head – metres

Fig. 10. MEASUREMENT OF FLOW OVER HORIZONTAL WEIRS

26

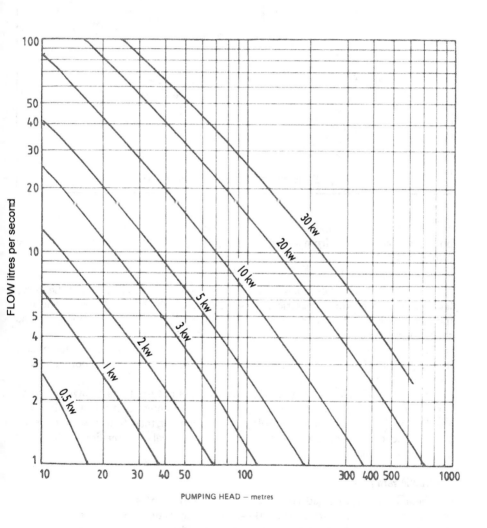

Fig. 11.   KILOWATT DEMAND OF PUMPS REQUIRED TO PROVIDE VARIOUS
FLOWS AT DIFFERENT PUMPING HEADS

27

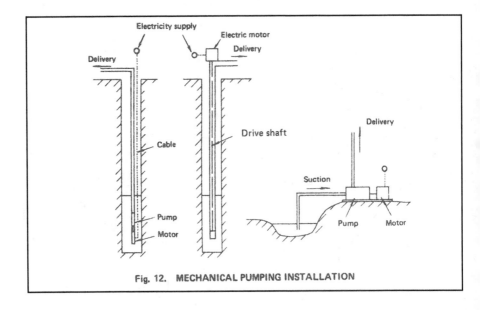

Fig. 12. MECHANICAL PUMPING INSTALLATION

centres. These are suitable when the pump suction has a positive pressure of water on it, but can be used from a shallow well or bore with a suction lift not exceeding 6 metres (20 ft).

b. Well pumps

In deeper wells or boreholes the pump itself must be situated below the water level. The drive motor, if electric, can be either fixed directly to the pump and submersed in the water (a submersible pump) or on the ground surface with a long shaft down to the pump, as shown in the sketches (Fig. 12).

For a submersible pump the rising main will be either screwed steel pipe or cast iron pipe with flanges. The electric cable will be lowered down the borehole with the rising main.

In the case of a shaft borehole pump, the pump shaft has to pass down the rising main with regularly placed special bearings. This requires careful installation, but the life of this type of pumping unit is usually greater than that of a submersible pump. The electric motor is then above ground level and readily available for routine maintenance.

Hydraulic ram pumps

These may be obtained commercially in a variety of sizes. The typical small commercial pump can lift 90 l/h (20 gal/h) to heights up to 60 m (200 ft) without consuming any external power excepting that derived from the water supply. An essential part of a ram pump installation is a metal drive pipe having about 24 cm length (9 inch) for every 30 cm (12 inch) of vertical height between the pump

28

and the final delivery point. This should be laid as straight as possible and be fed from a small dam. The column of water flowing down the pipe creates a water hammer effect which operates the valves in the pump, allowing about 10% of the total flow to be lifted to the required height: the remaining water then runs to waste. Ram pumps are costly and cannot be obtained in sizes small enough to suit very small communities. Small ram pumps may be built from steel pipe and standard fittings, requiring only the dash valve and the delivery valve to be made in a workshop. The design of ram pumps is empirical and some experimenting will be necessary to adjust the size and weight of the valves. A typical ram pump installation and a suggested design for a ram pump using standard pipe fittings is shown in Fig. 13.

Hand pumps

There are many commercially made hand pumps available at fairly low cost. Typical low-lift hand pumps will raise 35 l/min about 6 m height. The output will be increased as the height is decreased and vice versa. The maximum height that displacement pumps can lift is related to the atmospheric pressure so that at levels higher than sea level the maximum lifting height is reduced. Most commercial hand pumps are of the piston type or the semi-rotary type and are beyond the resources of most rural craftsmen to reproduce; however Fig. 14 shows a design of a displacement pump which could be constructed by many village craftsmen. It is essential that this type of pump should be of small size in order to remain within the capacity of manual operation, and only low lifts can be expected.

A hand pump of an entirely different type has been designed after the fashion of a ship's bilge pump. As this pump contains only one simple flap valve and no other moving parts it has been called the "Simplest pump". The method of construction and three methods of installation are shown in Fig. 15. The simplest pump is operated by raising and lowering the entire unit about 20 to 30 cm (8 to 12 inch) rhythmically at from 1 to 3 strokes per sec. Pumps up to 75 mm (3 inch) bore can lift 100 l/min (24 gal/min) from depths up to 4 m (13 ft) at up to 2000 m (6000 ft) above sea level. Simplest pumps can be built in sizes up to about 15 cm (6 inch) bore and can lift approximately 200 l/min from a depth of 1 m. A limiting factor in the ultimate size of simplest pumps is the weight which can be manually operated. This type of pump is most useful at lifts less than 3 m.

Rope lifts

The rope lift for water is simpler to build than any type of pump, is independent of height above sea level, and could be converted to bicycle power. A typical manual installation is shown in Fig. 16; pulleys can be hand made and the dimensions are not important. The rope can be of any diameter and almost any durable material. The operation of a rope lift depends on the rope being partly submerged in the water source and lifted over the pulleys at a rate faster than the water is flowing down the rope, thus the height of lift can be up to 20 m or more. The volume of

(Continued on p. 36).

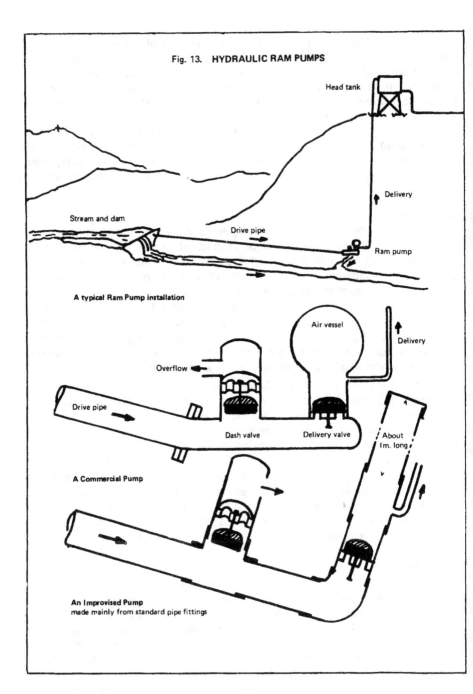

Fig. 13. HYDRAULIC RAM PUMPS

Head tank

Delivery

Stream and dam

Drive pipe

Ram pump

A typical Ram Pump installation

Air vessel

Delivery

Overflow

Drive pipe

Dash valve   Delivery valve   About
1m. long

A Commercial Pump

An Improvised Pump
made mainly from standard pipe fittings

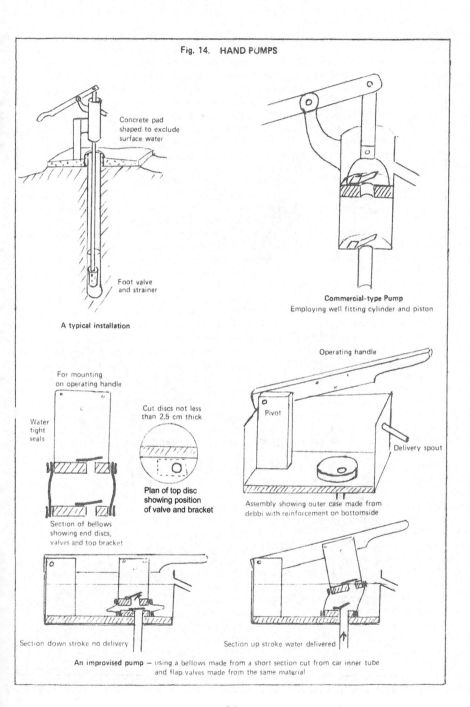

Fig. 14. HAND PUMPS

Concrete pad
shaped to exclude
surface water

Foot valve
and strainer

A typical installation

Commercial-type Pump
Employing well fitting cylinder and piston

Operating handle

For mounting
on operating handle

Water
tight
seals

Cut discs not less
than 2.5 cm thick

Pivot

Delivery spout

**Plan of top disc
showing position
of valve and bracket**

Assembly showing outer case made from
debbi with reinforcement on bottomside

Section of bellows
showing end discs,
valves and top bracket

Section down stroke no delivery

Section up stroke water delivered

An improvised pump — using a bellows made from a short section cut from car inner tube
and flap valves made from the same material

31

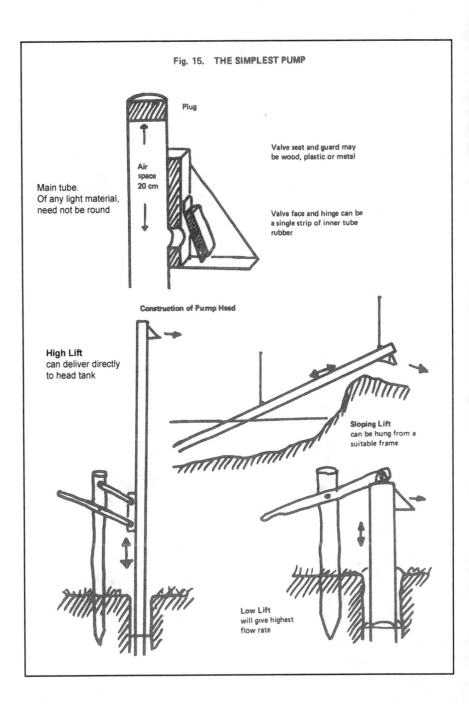

Fig. 15.   THE SIMPLEST PUMP

Plug

Valve seat and guard may
be wood, plastic or metal

Air
space
20 cm

Main tube.
Of any light material,
need not be round

Valve face and hinge can be
a single strip of inner tube
rubber

Construction of Pump Head

High Lift
can deliver directly
to head tank

Sloping Lift
can be hung from a
suitable frame

Low Lift
will give highest
flow rate

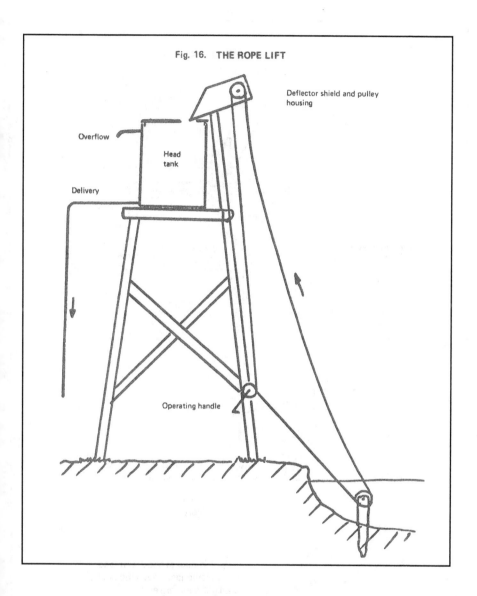

Fig. 16. **THE ROPE LIFT**

Deflector shield and pulley housing

Overflow

Head tank

Delivery

Operating handle

Fig. 17. BUCKET LIFTS IN SMALL WELLS

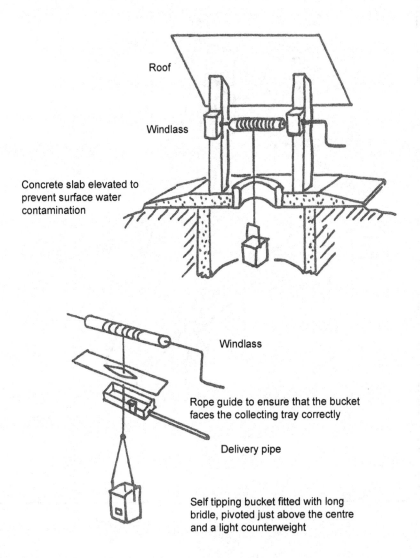

Roof

Windlass

Concrete slab elevated to
prevent surface water
contamination

Windlass

Rope guide to ensure that the bucket
faces the collecting tray correctly

Delivery pipe

Self tipping bucket fitted with long
bridle, pivoted just above the centre
and a light counterweight

A modification which can be fitted to a totally enclosed well head or may be adapted to deliver directly to a head tank.

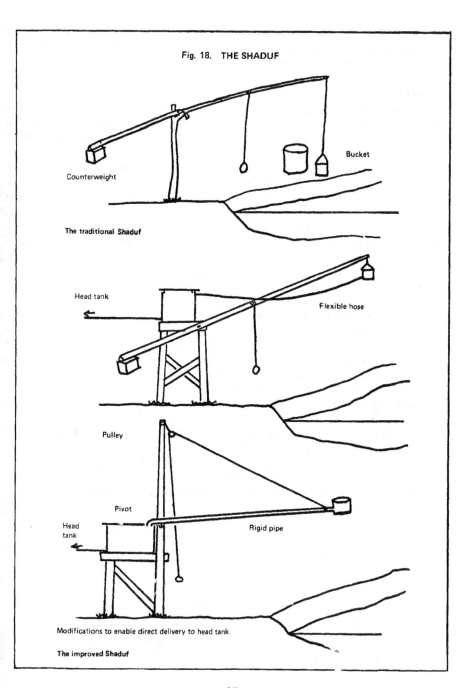

Fig. 18.   THE SHADUF

Counterweight

Bucket

The traditional Shaduf

Head tank

Flexible hose

Pulley

Pivot

Head
tank

Rigid pipe

Modifications to enable direct delivery to head tank

The improved Shaduf

water delivered depends on the surface area of the rope and the speed with which the apparatus is worked. Delivery rates of 15 l/min can be achieved by hand-driven lifts; cycle powered rope lifts can deliver more rapidly.

Bucket lifts

In the smallest rural communities with the minimum of resources, bucket lifts may be the only type of water-lifting device within their capacity to build. The windlass-operated well bucket is well known in rural areas in Europe and is illustrated in Fig. 17.

Care should be taken with bucket lifts to ensure that only the well bucket is dropped into the well and if removed it should not be placed on foul ground. Proper protection from surface water and if possible covers should be provided at wells. The self-emptying bucket types can be adapted to fill a head tank directly.

The traditional Arab 'shaduf' is a useful and simple device for lifting water but as it is not known in many other parts of rural Africa it is shown in Fig. 18 with a simple modification which will make transfer of water from the bucket more convenient. This type of self-emptying bucket can also be adapted to fill a head tank directly.

Special note on pumps and pipelines

Pumps and pipelines of the cheapest and simplest types may be all that is possible in some situations. If well made, well looked after and protected from neglect and abuse they can give good service for a long time. Even the best types of pumps and pipelines will fail if badly installed and neglected or abused. In many situations an immediate improvement in public health can occur when simple equipment is installed and properly used. Simple equipment can form a basis or nucleus from which the most efficient system can be developed as resources become available.

When using general charts for pipe design, such as those given in this chapter, it must be remembered that not all batches of similar class of pipe have exactly the same diameter or exactly the same roughness. Some allowance may need to be made for this. If pipe manufacturers provide charts specifically intended for their own pipes then those charts should be used rather than general charts.

Useful Factors

1 cu. ft. of water contains 6.24 gallons or 28.4 litres.
1 cu. metre of water contains 220 gallons.
1 gallon of water weighs 10 lb.
1 cu. foot per second = 540,000 gallons per day.
1 horse power =   550 ft lb/sec
            =   746 watts
For calculating horse power:

B.H.P. = $\dfrac{Flow\ (litres/sec)\ x\ pumping\ head\ (metres)\ x}{76}$ $\dfrac{100}{efficiency\ (\%)}$

kW = $\dfrac{Flow\ (litres/sec)\ x\ pumping\ head\ (metres)\ x}{102}$ $\dfrac{100}{efficiency\ (\%)}$

Metric Units

1 kg (kilogram) = 1000 g (gram) = 2.205 lb.
1 g (gram)   = 1000 mg (milligram)
1 l (litre)   = 1000 ml (millilitres) = 0.22 gal.
1 mg/1 = 1 milligram per litre – considering solutions of substances in water mg/l is approximately the same as parts per million (ppm or pp 10^6)
1 m (metre= 100 cm) = 1.094 yards
1 cm (centimetre) = 10 mm (millimetre)
2.54 cm = 1 inch
1 m^3 of water= 1000 l, weight 1000 kg. approximately 1 ton UK

Abbreviations

A.R. – analytical reagent, a high quality and very pure form of a chemical substance.
BOD – biochemical oxygen demand, see p. 63.
Cl2 – the chemists abbreviation for chlorine, it is also used to represent one molecule of chlorine.
E.coli – Escherichia coli, a common intestinal organism or bacterium. Its presence in a water supply indicates pollution from human or animal excreta and maybe accompanied by organisms of serious diseases.
Gal – gallon. Throughout this handbook the UK or Imperial gallon is used. Other publications may be found which use the US gallon which is not the same measure.

1 gal UK = 1.2003 gal US= 4.546 litres

SS – suspended solids, undissoived matter floating throughout the depth of water. SS maybe of animal, vegetable or mineral origin and a proportion is able to settle out.

37

Chapter Three

Water Treatment

The treatment of water for small communities can be considered in four sections:

a. Storage and settlement
b. Flocculation and settlement
c. Filtration
d. Disinfection or sterilization

Wherever possible all water supplied for public consumption should be free from harmful organisms. Many deep boreholes or well protected springs may provide water substantially free from microbiological impurities, this can be verified by bacteriological tests if possible. Most surface waters and shallow wells in tropical areas are exposed to faecal pollution by animals or people, and if such sources are used they should be disinfected or sterilized. It is usually cheaper and easier to supply good quality water that requires little or no treatment, than to treat polluted water which may be easier to obtain or to pump. Where disinfection is found to be necessary, proper care and regular chemical testing should be exercised at all times, as only one act of carelessness or folly can have serious consequences.

Most water supply installations embody some form of primary storage tank or pond and its value as a settlement tank cannot be under-estimated. Where there is a danger of bilharzia infection, if protected storage is introduced for a period of 48 hours the cercaria are unable to infect a host and will die. Some authorities consider that 36 hours is sufficient. Other organisms may be reduced in numbers by the same method, though for most bacteria, storage times in excess of a week are necessary to produce a significant reduction. Two weeks' storage can reduce bacteria populations by 50 to 90 per cent depending on the severity of pollution. Prolonged storage in uncovered tanks can produce thick algal growths and may encourage mosquito breeding; precautions must be taken to prevent these occurring. All storage tank inlets should be screened to prevent contamination by gross suspended matter and tanks should be covered to protect them from birds and small animals. Storage tanks may be constructed from steel, or excavated and if necessary lined with concrete, brick or with polythene film.

Flocculation and filtration may be required to remove further suspended solids and colour from the raw water to render it safe and acceptable in appearance for general use.

Flocculation requires the careful dosing of the raw water with chemicals and is considered beyond the scope of most small developments. It will however be dealt with in general terms.

Filtration is the passage of the water through a sand bed which will retain the suspended solids. Various methods of sand filtration will be outlined, some well tried on modern water treatment plants and others given here as suggestions for local development.

Flocculation and sedimentation

In order to increase the capacity of filtration plants, it is possible to coagulate suspended matter by the use of chemicals, and then allow the heavier particles to settle.

Coagulants:

1. Aluminium sulphate (sulphate of alumina, alum, aluminoferric) — often the only chemical available.
2. Sodium aluminate — usually used in conjunction with aluminium sulphate
3. Ferrous sulphate and lime
4. Ferric chloride

The choice and dose of these chemicals will depend on the characteristics of the water to be treated and can be found only by laboratory experiments on the raw water. The dose rate may be from 5 mg/l to 100 mg/l of coagulant.

The settlement of the heavier particles can take place in either horizontal or vertical flow tanks (Fig. 19). The sludge must be removed from the floor of horizontal tanks. In the case of vertical flow tanks the flocculated material can form a mass called a blanket which is held in position by the upward velocity of flow of the water. The blanket then acts as a further filter to aid the removal of the flocculated material. Coagulant solutions may be added to water by continuous doses (Fig. 20) if a reasonable uniform rate of flow is maintained.

It can easily be seen that flocculation and sedimentation require a large amount of initial capital expenditure on plant and tanks and then require continual chemical dosing and maintenance. The cost of any water thus produced is bound to be high.

Sand filtration

Many methods of sand filtration can be considered and each may have particular advantages for any one scheme.

1. Rapid sand filters

These can be either open tanks (rapid gravity filters Fig. 21) or closed metal tanks where the water passes through under pressure (pressure filters).

Water is supplied to the top of a bed of sand about 1 m (3 ft) deep supported on a layer of graded sand incorporating a system of underdrains. In order to maintain adequate flow an operating depth of water from 1½ to 2 m (5 to 6 ft) must be

39

Fig. 19. SEDIMENTATION TANKS

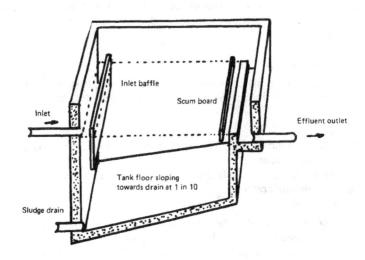

Inlet baffle

Scum board

Inlet

Effluent outlet

Tank floor sloping
towards drain at 1 in 10

Sludge drain

Horizontal flow type

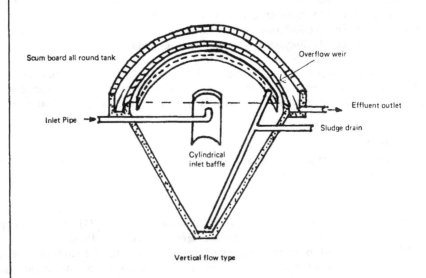

Scum board all round tank

Overflow weir

Inlet Pipe

Effluent outlet

Sludge drain

Cylindrical
inlet baffle

Vertical flow type

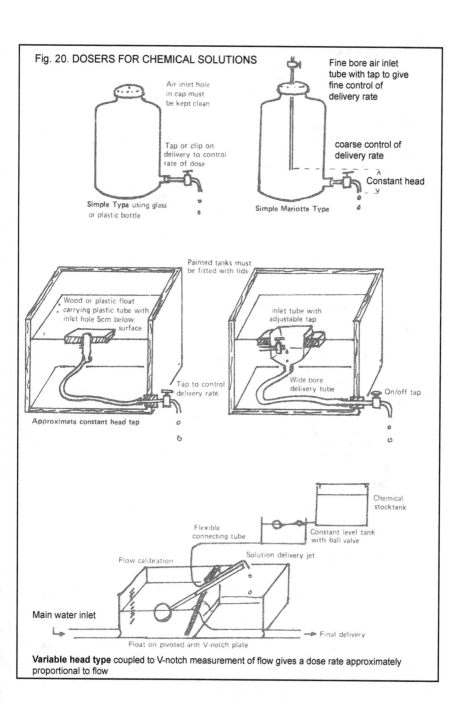

Fig. 20. DOSERS FOR CHEMICAL SOLUTIONS

Air inlet hole
in cap must
be kept clean

Fine bore air inlet
tube with tap to give
fine control of
delivery rate

Tap or clip on
delivery to control
rate of dose

coarse control of
delivery rate

Constant head

Simple Type using glass
or plastic bottle

Simple Mariotte Type

Painted tanks must
be fitted with lids

Wood or plastic float
carrying plastic tube with
inlet hole 5cm below
surface

inlet tube with
adjustable tap

Tap to control
delivery rate

Wide bore
delivery tube

On/off tap

Approximate constant head tap

Chemical
stocktank

Flexible
connecting tube

Constant level tank
with ball valve

Solution delivery jet

Flow calibration

Main water inlet

Final delivery

Float on pivoted arm V-notch plate

Variable head type coupled to V-notch measurement of flow gives a dose rate approximately
proportional to flow

41

maintained above the sand. The total through-put can be as much as 2400 to 7200 litres per m² (50 to 150 gallons per sq. ft) per hour. The filtering action of the rapid sand filter is entirely mechanical and suspended matter is accumulated in the voids until the through-put drops to an inadequate level. At this point it is necessary to clean the filter by backwashing with filtered water and frequently by agitating the sand bed mechanically or with compressed air.

The necessity for frequent backwashing requires trained staff and frequent checking. However a rapid gravity filter is compact and efficient and is very suitable for large installations on restricted sites.

When used in conjunction with sedimentation and flocculation, almost any water can be clarified by rapid sand filtration. Professional advice is however required before any work of this nature is undertaken.

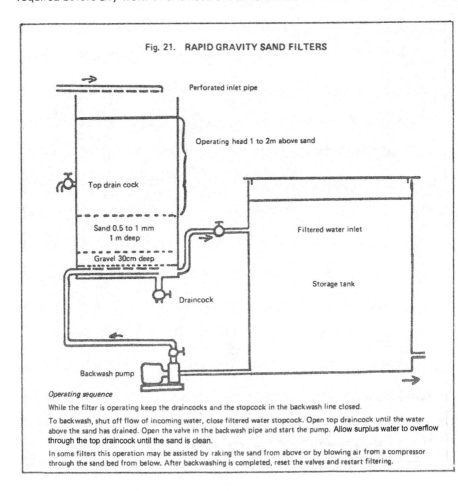

Fig. 21. RAPID GRAVITY SAND FILTERS

Perforated inlet pipe

Operating head 1 to 2m above sand

Top drain cock

Sand 0.5 to 1 mm
1 m deep

Gravel 30cm deep

Filtered water inlet

Draincock

Storage tank

Backwash pump

Operating sequence

While the filter is operating keep the draincocks and the stopcock in the backwash line closed.

To backwash, shut off flow of incoming water, close filtered water stopcock. Open top draincock until the water above the sand has drained. Open the valve in the backwash pipe and start the pump. Allow surplus water to overflow through the top draincock until the sand is clean.

In some filters this operation may be assisted by raking the sand from above or by blowing air from a compressor through the sand bed from below. After backwashing is completed, reset the valves and restart filtering.

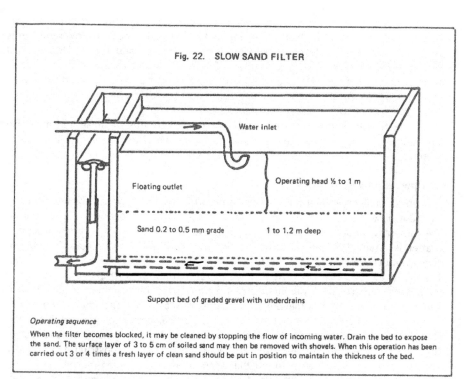

Fig. 22. SLOW SAND FILTER

Water inlet

Operating head ½ to 1 m

Floating outlet

Sand 0.2 to 0.5 mm grade   1 to 1.2 m deep

Support bed of graded gravel with underdrains

Operating sequence

When the filter becomes blocked, it may be cleaned by stopping the flow of incoming water. Drain the bed to expose the sand. The surface layer of 3 to 5 cm of soiled sand may then be removed with shovels. When this operation has been carried out 3 or 4 times a fresh layer of clean sand should be put in position to maintain the thickness of the bed.

2. Slow sand filters

The structure of a slow sand filter is similar to a rapid sand filter in that water is supplied to the surface of a bed of sand of somewhat smaller particle size, about 0.2 to 0.5 mm and about 1.2 m (4 ft) deep supported on a bed of graded gravel incorporating an underdrain system (Fig. 22). An operating depth of about ½ to 1 m (2 to 3 ft) of water must be maintained above the sand level and the rate of flow restricted to about 100 litres per m^2 (2 gallons per sq. ft) per hour. Initially the filtering action of a slow sand filter is the same as that of a rapid filter but suspended matter accumulates at the surface of the sand layer and in a short time a layer of living organisms forms which adds a significant biological purifying contribution to the mechanical filtering action. This enables colloidal material to be removed and the bacterial counts of the raw water are reduced considerably. Dissolved inorganic and organic material is also consumed by the biological film, resulting in some improvement to colour. The slow sand filter cannot be back-washed in the same way as the rapid filter and when cleaning becomes necessary, much less frequently than with rapid filters, the soiled surface of the sand is exposed by draining and must be manually removed to a depth of 1 or 2 inches. A freshly cleaned bed requires a little time to re-establish treatment so that some duplicate equipment must be installed in a slow sand filter plant. The advantages

43

of slow sand filters lie in their great simplicity. The maintenace of slow sand filters is simple and requires less critical attention than rapid sand filters. No chemical dosing is necessary with slow sand filters. The serious disadvantage of the slow sand filter is that it requires 40 to 50 times the land area of a rapid filter with the same through-put. In rural situations where space and labour are not serious considerations, this type of plant offers many advantages.

In the tropics exposed water may grow dense growths of algae and may also encourage mosquito breeding. Precautions should be taken to control these diffifulties.

3. Upward-flow sand filters

Considerable experimental work has been carried out on upward-flow sand filters. In these, raw water is introduced into a gravel layer supporting a bed of coarse 3-4 mm sand about 30 cm (1 ft) deep. In its passage upwards, coarse suspended matter is retained in the lower part of the sand bed and finer material is progressively removed by the upper layers. The through-put must be restricted to prevent lifting of the sand. With most raw water rates of 500 to 1500 l/m^2 (10 to 30 gallons per square foot) per hour effect a significant improvement in quality and there is evidence that some biological activity is able to take place. The action is therefore a compromise between the mechanical action of a rapid filter and the biological and mechanical action of the slow filter. The major advantages offered by the upward-flow sand filter are, firstly simplicity of construction, secondly ease of cleaning. It has been found that accumulated suspended matter may be removed by simply stopping the input of raw water and rapidly lowering the level of water above the bed by draining, thus reversing the direction of flow. This operation is quick and easy and may be incorporated into a simple daily routine. This kind of filter thus offers advantages which make it particularly suited for many intermediate situations such as farm estates, schools or trading estates.

In practical terms an upward flow filter (Fig. 23) constructed from a 44 gallon oil drum with an area of 2.64 sq. ft would be capable of filtering some 225 litres (50 gallons) per hour or, if operated for 12 hours daily, of producing 2700 litres (600 gal) per day. The cost of such a filter is little more than the cost of the drum, a few pieces of pipe and a stop-cock. The maintenance of the filter is the ordinary routine cleaning of the filter by backwashing which might be a routine daily task. In larger sizes, common corrugated galvanised water tanks may be used; a 6ft (1.8 m) diameter tank would have an output of 2500 litres per hour (560 gals/hour) at the same loading.

4. Horizontal sand filter

This simple method of filtration, a modification of the slow sand filter, is of Dutch origin where use is made of the large areas of sand dunes which consist of good quality filter sand in thick layers over impervious clay. This enables impure water to be pumped into the sand at high points. The water is allowed to

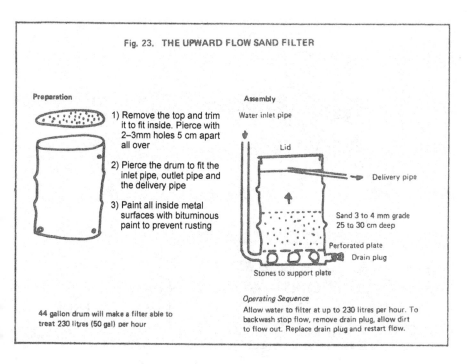

Fig. 23. THE UPWARD FLOW SAND FILTER

Preparation

1) Remove the top and trim it to fit inside. Pierce with 2–3mm holes 5 cm apart all over

2) Pierce the drum to fit the inlet pipe, outlet pipe and the delivery pipe

3) Paint all inside metal surfaces with bituminous paint to prevent rusting

44 gallon drum will make a filter able to treat 230 litres (50 gal) per hour

Assembly

Water inlet pipe

Lid

Delivery pipe

Sand 3 to 4 mm grade 25 to 30 cm deep

Perforated plate

Drain plug

Stones to support plate

Operating Sequence

Allow water to filter at up to 230 litres per hour. To backwash stop flow, remove drain plug, allow dirt to flow out. Replace drain plug and restart flow.

percolate through the sand by the influence of the head and the permeability of the sand and it can be collected at lower points in the dunes substantially purified. The retention period in the dunes in Holland is often as much as 30 days. This allows the organic matter which accumulates in the sand to be oxidized to carbon dioxide by natural biological action.

This system of filtration offers many advantages to rural tropical communities as construction costs are low and maintenance is minimal. The higher tropical temperatures would favour biological activity. Filtration by this method enables large quantities of water to be filtered with only a small area of exposed water surface, thus the risk of mosquito breeding or snail infection is reduced to proportions which make protective measures possible. Although the quantities of sand used are large compared with conventional filtration the cost of extra sand is not great on the scale that this would be adopted in rural conditions.

It is a comparatively easy type of filter to construct in its simplest form (Fig.24) consisting of a bed or channel cut into the ground, lined with polythene film to provide a water seal and filled with suitable clean sand of 10 to 52 mesh (0.07 to 0.01 in. or 1.85 to 0.25 mm). Raw water is allowed to flow into a small depression at one end of the channel, and a second depression about 10 to 13 m (30 or 40 ft) away at a lower level giving an effective slope of about 1 in 20 allows filtered water to flow out. The retention time in such filters should be of the order of 36 hours or more. Since the water-holding capacity or voids capacity of sand is usually

45

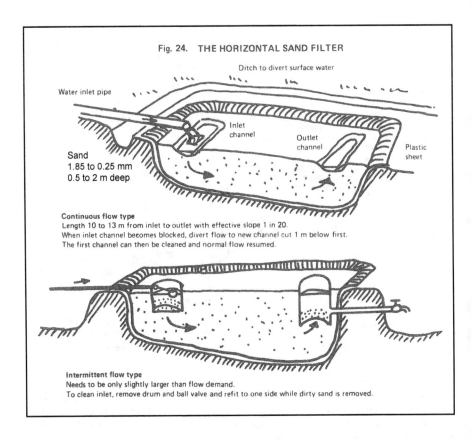

Fig. 24. THE HORIZONTAL SAND FILTER

Ditch to divert surface water

Water inlet pipe

Inlet channel

Outlet channel

Plastic sheet

Sand
1.85 to 0.25 mm
0.5 to 2 m deep

Continuous flow type
Length 10 to 13 m from inlet to outlet with effective slope 1 in 20.
When inlet channel becomes blocked, divert flow to new channel cut 1 m below first.
The first channel can then be cleaned and normal flow resumed.

Intermittent flow type
Needs to be only slightly larger than flow demand.
To clean inlet, remove drum and ball valve and refit to one side while dirty sand is removed.

about 40 per cent, the volume of sand required may be calculated as follows:

$$\text{Volume of sand} = \text{daily output required} \times \frac{36}{24} \times \frac{100}{40}$$

The action of the horizontal sand filter to some extent resembles that of the slow sand filter. A skin develops on the surface of the sand at the influent point but the rate of application at this point is much greater than that of a slow sand filter so that biological activity takes place within the body of the filter and if sufficient retention time is allowed then the biological action is completed and the final water is of good bacteriological quality.

Results from practical field tests may be briefly summarised as follows. Two widely differing types of water have been treated by horizontal sand filtration and in both cases about 75 per cent of the polluting impurities have been removed in less than the retention time recommended. Beds of about 2¼ cubic metres of sand are able to deliver about 25 to 50 litres of water per hour (6-12 gal/hr) depending

46

on the permeability of the sand. On a continuous flow basis this would provide 600 to 1200 litres per day (150-300 gal/day) or sufficient for a rural population of 13 to 26 people assuming a consumption of 45 litres per person per day. This would fit a great many rural situations. If more water is required the filter can easily be extended even after it has been in use for a time.

Iron removal (Fig. 25)

Many swamp waters and some borehole waters contain insoluble and dissolved iron compounds which are objectionable in water supplies. The most usual soluble iron compounds found are ferrous sulphate or ferrous bicarbonate. At pH values over 7.0 these compounds can be removed by settlement or filtration. Sometimes exposure to the atmosphere in primary storage tanks enables sufficient oxidation to take place to remove low concentrations of iron. More efficient iron removal can be accomplished by aerating the water. This can be easily carried out by allowing the water, after treatment with limestone to raise the pH value if necessary, to trickle through layers of broken stone or gravel about 2.5 cm mesh and 15 cm deep. Two or more layers may be necessary separated by air spaces. If coke can be obtained it often performs more efficiently than gravel or rock. It may be worth experimenting with hard charcoal broken into suitable sizes. The rate of application of water to this kind of filter is approximately 1600 l/m^2/h. Iron compounds may also be precipitated by chlorine and some other chemicals but

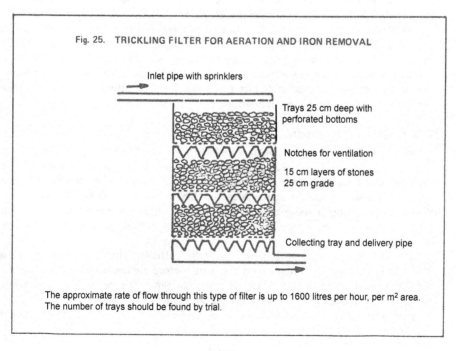

Fig. 25.   TRICKLING FILTER FOR AERATION AND IRON REMOVAL

Inlet pipe with sprinklers

Trays 25 cm deep with perforated bottoms

Notches for ventilation

15 cm layers of stones 25 cm grade

Collecting tray and delivery pipe

The approximate rate of flow through this type of filter is up to 1600 litres per hour, per m^2 area. The number of trays should be found by trial.

47

these processes require more control than is likely in rural areas. The trickling device described for iron precipitation aerates the water and may have beneficial effects on taste and odour.

5. Correction of acidity

Many tropical waters are acidic and have a very low pH value which, apart from direct undesirable effects, produces considerable corrosion in metal fittings with resulting secondary pollution by metal compounds. Also in many cases where alum flocculation is carried out the pH value of the raw water is below the level which will permit the alum floc to form. One method used to correct this is direct dosing of proportional quantities of lime with the alum. In many simple installations pH correction can be carried out by upward flow treatment through beds of crushed limestone (calcium carbonate). This has the advantage that since the practical limit of pH achieved is about 7.5 no dosing apparatus or control is necessary. In addition if the limestone is graded to a suitable size the bed may be incorporated in an upward-flow sand filter removing suspended matter. If the raw water contains a high concentration of sulphate the surface of the limestone may become coated after a time with insoluble calcium sulphate which will seriously impede the action. In such cases accurate dosing with lime slurries may be employed. The neutralization of the acids in the raw water results in some consumption of calcium carbonate but in a typical tropical situation the uptake of limestone was about 10 kg per million litres (100 lb per million gallons) and the hardness of the raw water was raised from 39 to 75 which still remains very soft.

Alkaline waters with high pH values cannot be corrected by this method but they are invariably associated with other conditions which make flocculation necessary. A by-product of flocculation with alum is the production of acid which reduces high pH values automatically. Alternatively, high pH values can be corrected by adding mineral acids but this should not be attempted unless proper testing and control can be maintained.

Disinfection or Sterilization

It is essential that public water supplies should be bacteriologically as safe as possible. Some deep well waters are naturally safe, but most surface waters are polluted and should be sterilized if possible. This is usually carried out by chlorination, with chlorine gas in some large supplies exceeding 25000 litres per hour. Small supplies find it more convenient to use solutions of chemicals containing free chlorine such as bleaching powder, chlorinated lime, sodium hypochlorite or HTH.

The chlorine dosing equipment should be sufficient firstly to allow not less than thirty minutes of contact with the water before use and secondly to maintain a chlorine residual of at least 0.3 mg/l after that time. The methods of estimating the dose and measuring the residual are set out earlier in this handbook.

Bleaching powder, or chlorinated lime, calcium hypochlorite, contains 35 per cent available chlorine by weight. Thus 1 Kg of powder will give 1,000 000 litres of water a dose of 0.35 mg/l, or 1 lb. of powder to 100 000 gallons a dose of 0.35 mg/l.

Commercial sodium hypochlorite solution contains 0.25 Kg per litre (2.5 lb. per gallon) of available chlorine. Thus 1 litre of commercial solution will provide 1 000 000 litres of water with 0.25 mg/l.

Dry HTH contains 70% by weight available chlorine. Thus 1 Kg will provide 1 000 000 litres with a dose of 0.7 mg/l or 1 lb in 100 000 gallons at 0.7 mg/l of chlorine.

Chlorine dosing

In order to obtain a constant chlorine dose with simple plant it is essential to dose into a constant flow, such as the flow from a pump, and not into a flow which is varying. Dosing on the inlet to a storage tank will often give this condition together with the necessary contact time before consumption.

A simple dosing apparatus can be made from a container such as a large plastic drum or a metal drum which has been painted inside with bituminous paint to protect the metal from corrosion (Fig. 20). A rubber delivery tube fitted to the bottom of the drum will enable the solution to be delivered to the water. The rate of delivery can be reduced with some suitable form of tap or a clamp squeezing the tube. A more uniform rate of delivery can be achieved if the liquid is allowed to flow out of the drum through a second tube inside the drum attached to a float which will keep the open end a constant depth below the surface of the liquid. This type of doser can be used for flocculants and other chemicals if required. If chloride of lime is used, it is essential to stir the solution occasionally to prevent settlement of the solid matter. Alternatively a stock solution can be prepared containing 100 g/l, allowed to settle and the clear top solution drawn off for use. Solutions made in this way retain their strength, maintaining about 18 gm/l of available chlorine for up to 48 hours.

It has been shown that to ensure a complete sterilization of bilharzia cercaria in a water of pH 7 it is necessary to have a chlorine residual of 0.5 mg/l after 30 minutes contact. If the pH of the water is increased from 7.0 to 8.5 this period of contact should be increased to 45 minutes to ensure safety.

All new mains and water works plant should be sterilized with a dose of chlorine of at least 25 mg/l and thoroughly flushed out before use.

Chlorine demand and residual

A simple equation defines the various terms:
Chlorine demand plus chlorine residual equals chlorine dose.

The chlorine residual has already been fixed and so the dose then varies with the chlorine demand, or degree of impurity.

The chlorine residual can be measured by the methods described on page 9 which can easily be carried out in the field.

Boiling

The boiling of water for a few minutes does not necessarily give complete sterilization. Although the majority of bacteria and virus are rendered harmless very rapidly, it is necessary to boil water for 20 minutes to ensure full safety.

Chapter Four

Foul Water and Excreta Disposal

The first step in waste collection and disposal is the provision of some kind of latrine system. Two important factors must be taken into account. The first is to consider whether to install communal facilities or facilities for every individual family. Factors influencing this choice are urgency and cheapness; if both needs are acute, communal latrines at least for most of the community are preferable. Communal latrines are however liable to neglect or abuse and regular inspection is necessary. Individual family latrines are preferable wherever possible, though in many kinds of rural community a degree of inspection will still be necessary. The second important factor dominating the design of latrine systems is the type of apparatus best suited to local customs. In many underdeveloped rural communities a squatting position is adopted and for this purpose a simple form of squatting plate can be provided. The simple squatting plate can have a toilet bowl added as required, or it may be replaced by suitable high level toilets in most systems.

In many areas piped water supplies are not available. Water-carriage sewerage systems are therefore not practical and the pit privy will be used. In some areas night soil bucket closets are used but these are expensive to maintain, requiring a kind of labour which is becoming increasingly difficult to recruit. Considering other sanitary objections to the system there are no grounds for recommending night soil bucket closets: they should be discouraged and are not described.

The pit privy

Unless it is intended to construct watertight pit privies the location of this type of privy should be considered in relation to the position of local water sources. In normal dry soil bacterial pollution from the contents of a non-watertight pit can migrate up to 7.5 m horizontally and 3 m vertically. If the water table is penetrated bacterial pollution can travel up to 30 m in the direction of flow of the ground water. If a well penetrates the water table it will induce water flow towards it so that the minimum distance permissible between an unsealed pit privy and a well or a stream used as a water source should be not less than 30 m, though the risk of infection beyond 20 m is small; in gravel or fissured rock the distances should be considerably increased. The minimum safe distance in fissured rock depends very much on the local physical conditions of the rock and no minimum safe distance can be usefully quoted. Under no circumstances should the distance be less than

200 m. Under the worst conditions bacterial contamination has been known to travel 2000 m. Local experience should be consulted in inhabited areas and if necessary pit privies should be made watertight or an alternative system employed. Pits should not be sited at a higher level than wells. To ensure regular use and cleaning they should be sited close to dwellings, but not less than 5 m in most circumstances. In some circumstances very small pit privies are used but they are only suitable for temporary camps or emergency facilities. There are two types of pit privy suitable for regular use: the basic pit and the borehole pit.

The basic pit privy

This consists of a manually dug hole, round or rectangular in cross section, not less than 2.5 m (8 ft) deep. The minimum practical diameter to permit digging is about 1 m. Some revetement may be necessary at least near the mouth of the pit if there is any likelihood of soil collapsing. The volume of the pit is related to its useful life; under average conditions for a pit which penetrates the ground water table and is consequently permanently wet, a capacity of approximately 40 litres capacity per person per year should be allowed, assuming no bulky cleansing materials such as grass, leaves or similar materials are used.

In circumstances where such materials are commonly used, the capacity per person per year should be increased to 60 litres. In practice pits should have a storage period of not less than 1½ years, preferably more than 4 years. A pit privy is considered to be full to capacity when the contents reach a level 50 cm from ground level. At this point the pit should be filled with earth and the contents allowed to decompose for about 1 year, when the digested material can be removed and spread on land without offence. No disinfectants should be added to pit privies as they will prevent biological action and create offence.

The superstructure of a pit can vary to suit circumstances. A simple wooden floor with a hole for the user surrounded by a simple shelter is not uncommon in many areas. This may be improved upon by introducing properly designed squatting plates cast in concrete on a scale of one for every 10-12 users and equipped with covers to minimize fly breeding. A simple high level closet, comprising a seat, lid and drop pipe, can be installed and the shelter can be made as elaborate as required. An essential precaution is the prevention of surface water entering the pit by suitably elevating the floor. Mosquito breeding can be prevented by the weekly addition of a small quantity of oil. A diagram illustrating a pit privy and suitable types of squatting plate and cover, and pour flush closet is shown in Fig. 26.

The less common water-tight pit privy should be in general similar in design to the unsealed pit but functions more like a cess pit and should have an accordingly larger capacity, usually about 500 litres per person per year. Watertight pits should not be used unless an adequate emptying and disposal service can be provided.

The water-seal closet (pour flush)

A type of closet which uses a modified squatting plate embodying a small closet bowl with a very shallow water seal has proved popular in many parts of the Far

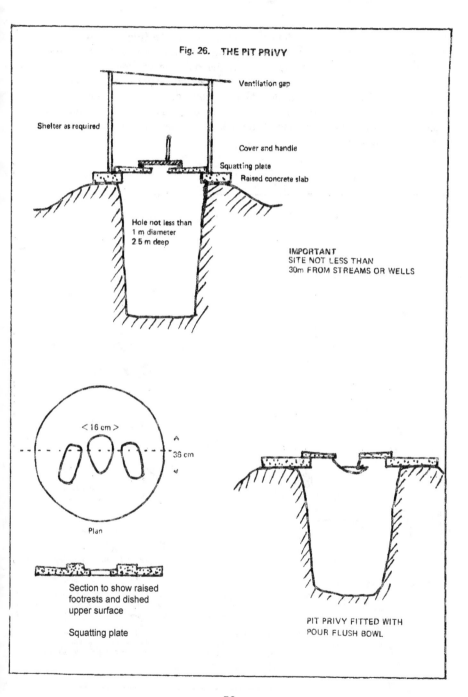

Fig. 26.   THE PIT PRIVY

Ventilation gap

Shelter as required

Cover and handle

Squatting plate

Raised concrete slab

Hole not less than
1 m diameter
2 5 m deep

IMPORTANT
SITE NOT LESS THAN
30m FROM STREAMS OR WELLS

< 16 cm >

36 cm

Plan

Section to show raised
footrests and dished
upper surface

Squatting plate

PIT PRIVY FITTED WITH
POUR FLUSH BOWL

53

East and may sometimes be found in southern Europe (Fig. 27). As it embodies a water seal it removes all problems of fly and mosquito breeding and all possibility of odour nuisance from the contents of the pit. The volume of water used for flushing may be as low as 1½ litres. Water-seal closets may be cast in concrete as an integral part of the squatting plate which for convenience should be circular so that it may be easily rolled into position. It may be possible to use a similar type of bowl in a normal high level closet though it will need to be deeper and require rather more flushing water.

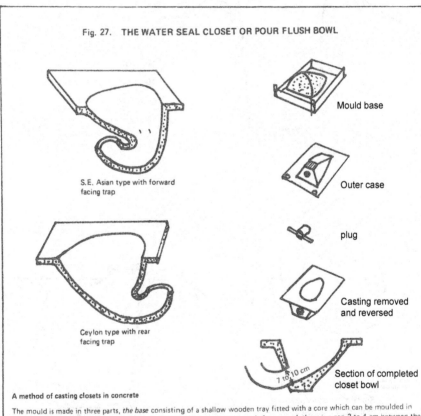

Fig. 27.   THE WATER SEAL CLOSET OR POUR FLUSH BOWL

S.E. Asian type with forward facing trap

Ceylon type with rear facing trap

Mould base

Outer case

plug

Casting removed and reversed

7 to 10 cm

Section of completed closet bowl

A method of casting closets in concrete

The mould is made in three parts, *the base* consisting of a shallow wooden tray fitted with a core which can be moulded in concrete, and two locating pegs. Fitting over the base is *the outer case* made from wood, there is a gap 3 to 4 cm between the base and the outer case, which is fitted with *the plug* which forms the hole for the outlet pipe. All inside surfaces of the mould are greased before casting.

Concrete made from 2½ parts sand and 1 part cement is rammed into the mould through the filling hole and allowed to set for 24 hours. The plug and the case can then be removed, and after a further 24 hours the bowl can be carefully lifted from the base and allowed to harden for about 4 or 5 days. The bowl is completed by cementing a standard pipe elbow of the correct size into the hole left by the plug.

54

The use of a water-seal closet makes it possible to install the closet in the house, connected to the pit by a pipe 100 to 150 mm bore laid in a straight run for as short a distance as possible at a slope not less than 1 in 20. Using this system more than one closet can be connected to a single pit.

If a water-seal closet is mounted directly over a pit, the wall of the pit directly opposite the closet discharge should be protected to prevent erosion.

The borehole pit

This type of pit differs from the basic pit mainly by its method of construction. An earth auger not less than 40 cm diameter is used to bore a hole not less than 4 m deep and up to the limit of the auger depth (10 m). The superstructure and function are exactly the same as the basic pit though the capacity is invariably less, thus the life of a borehole pit is less. Owing to the narrowness of the borehole, soiling of the upper walls takes place, increasing the danger of fly breeding. If a borehole is drilled into a water table subject to fairly rapid fluctuations a scum layer may bridge the bore and reduce its effective capacity unless broken by rodding from above.

If suitable augers are available the construction of borehole pits in normal soils is very simple and rapid, and if constructed in pairs a few feet apart, the superstructure can be transferred easily from the full hole to the empty hole thus establishing continuity. Some success has been had in parts of India with boreholes 15 cm diameter and 2 m deep which can be dug in about 30 minutes. In normally porous soils the life of these pits is seldom more than 4 or 5 months for a family of 6 people.

The aqua privy

A properly designed aqua privy which is kept clean can be partially installed within a dwelling. It consists of a water-tight tank to receive wastes in which biological activity resembling that in a septic tank takes place. An effluent is produced which must be properly disposed of in soak pits or by secondary treatment. Solids accumulate in the tank which must be removed at intervals.

The design of a typical aqua privy installation is shown in Fig. 28. In this design a simple drop is used to convey wastes from the squatting plate to the tank. It is convenient if the pipe is not firmly cemented in position so that it can be removed if necessary to clear blockages. Where a drop pipe is fitted it should be flushed after use with about 1.5 litres of water. The water-seal bowl may also be fitted to an aqua privy and is somewhat easier to keep clean. Tanks of adequate size may be fitted with a number of drop pipes in communal toilets.

The tank can be a single chamber tank but the settlement of solids from the effluent is invariably improved by adopting a two-tank design. The total capacity of the aqua privy is determined by the number of users and the desirable frequency of desludging. A suitable formula for calculating volume has been derived.

55

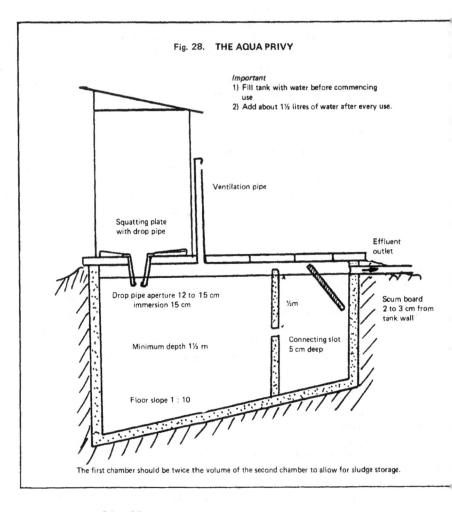

Fig. 28.   THE AQUA PRIVY

Important
1) Fill tank with water before commencing use
2) Add about 1½ litres of water after every use.

Ventilation pipe

Squatting plate with drop pipe

Effluent outlet

Drop pipe aperture 12 to 15 cm immersion 15 cm

½m

Scum board 2 to 3 cm from tank wall

Minimum depth 1½ m

Connecting slot 5 cm deep

Floor slope 1 : 10

The first chamber should be twice the volume of the second chamber to allow for sludge storage.

$$V = PQ + SP$$

where   V = volume
P = number of users
Q = volume of liquid discharged per person per day 9 to 12 litres.
S = volume of sludge storage space allowed per person, a reasonable factor is 120 to 150 litres

A minimum recommended volume for aqua privies is about 1500 litres which will serve up to 10 people.

Aqua privies may be used as communal toilets where somewhat smaller volume allowances per person may be used.

To commission a new aqua privy it must first be filled with water to make the water seal at the drop pipe and if possible, a few buckets of sludge from an established privy or septic tank added to the first compartment. When in regular use disinfectants should not be added to aqua privies as they will stop the biological action though small quantities of lime or chloride of lime can be tolerated from time to time. No solid matter which might cause blockage should be put in an aqua privy. If the aqua privy is unused for a time then one or more bucketfuls of water should be added daily to maintain flow through the system.

The sludge which accumulates must be removed when it reaches to within 10 or 15 cm of the connecting aperture between the two chambers. The level can be established with a sounding rod about every 3 months. Sludge removal will not be necessary in a properly designed tank at intervals of less than about 5 years. It may be buried or composted, but as it contains some undigested faecal matter should not be spread on the surface of land without treatment. As a guide to the size of soak pits required for effluent disposal, a trench should be constructed 1 m deep and 30 cm wide with a gradient of 1 in 30 containing 50 cm depth of crushed rock and built 1 to 1½ m in length for every person and backfilled with soil. When desludging aqua privies some sludge should be retained to seed the privy when it is refilled with water for further use.

Septic tanks

The septic tank is designed to accept all liquid wastes from a dwelling including kitchen waste and bathroom waste. Septic tanks commonly used for populations up to 300 persons in temperate climates are designed to accept liquid flows of about 180 litres per person per day; the volume of waste waters produced in rural communities, especially in the tropics, is likely to be very much lower. Experiments have shown that the reduction of polluting matter carried out in septic tanks is approximately 50 per cent in temperate climates but is about 75 per cent in the tropics where sewage of a similar strength is treated. Furthermore owing to the higher ambient temperatures the biological action in septic tanks reaches its maximum more quickly than in temperate climates.

The general design of a typical septic tank installation is shown in Fig. 29. The critical design factor of the septic tank is its liquid volume.

Current practice in temperate climates uses the following formula

$$V = (180P + 2000) \text{ litres}$$
where V = total tank volume
P = number of users.

In areas where the flow rate of wastes is lower the same formula would give rise to longer retention times which are of no benefit and result in septic tanks being built uneconomically large in size. A more suitable formula for the tropics is as follows:

$$V = PQ + SP$$
where V = volume

57

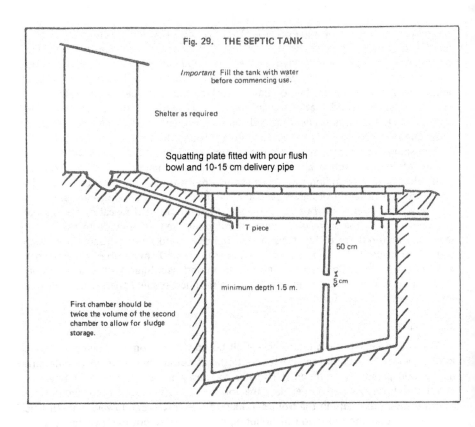

Fig. 29. THE SEPTIC TANK

Important Fill the tank with water before commencing use.

Shelter as required

Squatting plate fitted with pour flush bowl and 10-15 cm delivery pipe

T piece

50 cm

5 cm

minimum depth 1.5 m.

First chamber should be twice the volume of the second chamber to allow for sludge storage.

P = number of users
Q = volume of water discharged/person/day
S = volume of sludge storage, 120 to 150 litres per head is a reasonable figure.

This formula assumes a retention time of 24 hours and a minimum V of 1500 litres

Septic tanks may be connected to water-seal closets or the normal type of high-level closet and all other sources of domestic waste waters such as baths, showers, kitchens, etc., but on no account should roof drainage or surface water drainage be allowed to enter the septic tank system. Effluents from septic tanks and aqua privies can be discharged directly to large water-courses with adequate flow or to soak pits. If neither of these methods is possible further treatment must be carried out as described in Chapter 5. Septic tanks should be filled with water before commissioning. A few bucketfuls of sludge from an established septic tank will accelerate the start of biological action. When desludging septic tanks some sludge should be allowed to remain and the tank refilled with water. Desludging must be carried out when the level of sludge determined with a sounding rod rises to within 10 to 15 cm of the connecting aperture between the two chambers of the septic tank. Frequency of sludge removal may be of the order of 3 to 5 years subject to local conditions. Sludge may be disposed of in the same manner recommended for aqua privy sludge.

Septic tanks and aqua privies are often unfairly condemned because they fail some time after installing. There are three main causes of failure in these systems.

1. If insufficient water is added the water seals fail, due to evaporation, bad smells occur and no effluent is discharged.

2. If tanks are not desludged at the proper time, sludge can discharge with the effluent and cause blockages in soak pits. Neglect of sludge disposal can result in whole systems clogging and overflowing causing severe nuisance and health hazards.

3. Effluent disposal in soak pits or drainfields must be properly designed. Systems that are too small or are sited in impermeable soil will inevitably clog and overflow.

Proper maintenance in good time is essential for the effective working of all systems.

Area requirements for drainfields

Effluents discharged to subsurface drains are distributed along the whole length of the drain, seep through the rockfill to the floor of the drain then soak away through the soil surface. If this surface becomes clogged the drainage field will fail. The design of drainfields therefore depends on the volume of effluent discharged, which must, above all else, be free from solid matter; on the permeability of the soil; and on the floor area of the drains.

Permeability can be measured by digging a test hole about 250mm below the level of the proposed discharge. The hole is then filled with clean water and allowed to drain. Next day the test hole can be refilled to a depth of at least 250 mm and allowed to drain for a measured period of time. The levels of water before and after the test can be measured with a dipstick and the rate of draining in seconds per mm can be measured. This procedure is repeated 2 or 3 times. The average rate in seconds per mm is called the percolation value. Values greater than 140 secs indicate soil unsuitable for drainfields; conditions are best where values are less than 100 secs.

The percolation value can be used to calculate the floor area of trenches in the drainfield from the following formula:

$$\text{Area (m}^2\text{)} = \frac{\text{population served} \times \text{percolation value}}{4}$$

This area is suitable for population discharging 100 litres of effluent per person per day. If the discharge is widely different the area should be increased or decreased pro rata.

Chapter Five

Sewage Treatment

Aqua privies and septic tanks together with an adequate means of final effluent disposal, may be all that is required in small sewerage systems. Larger systems, serving populations exceeding 200 to 300, may require secondary treatment of the effluents before discharge. This may include many of the established methods of sewage treatment, and therefore may be adopted to include untreated domestic wastes directly from water closets, kitchens and bathrooms.

Sewerage schemes of this nature will require a properly laid system of sewers. Pressure pipes described in Chapter 2 for water supply systems can be used for gravity sewerage systems, but salt-glazed pipes and concrete pipes are generally cheaper in large sizes. Concrete pipes, usually in longer lengths than salt-glazed pipes can sometimes be manufactured locally. These pipes should preferably be of the spigot and socket type with flexible rubber ring joints although pipes for mortared joints may be more readily available. Thin-walled PVC pipe may also be available in suitable sizes.

An essential preliminary to any process for the treatment of raw sewage is the removal of gross solids, rag, paper, leaves, etc. which may cause physical blockages. A simple screen consisting of a grill of vertical bars set 2.5 to 3.5 cm apart will often suffice. In most small installations screens may be fitted just prior to the first stage of treatment. It is envisaged that a treatment plant, on the scale now being discussed, will have at least a part-time attendant responsible for routine maintenance. An important part of his duties is the periodic removal of accumulated solids from the bar screen with a rake. Neglect of this will allow blockages to form and may cause serious offence.

Sedimentation

Much of the polluting matter in raw sewage is in the form of suspended insoluble particles which can be settled out in suitably designed sedimentation tanks; if the sewage is derived from aqua privy or septic tank effluents no sedimentation tanks are needed. There are two main types of sedimentation tank, upward-flow and horizontal-flow. The simplest type to build is the horizontal-flow type (Fig. 19). It should have a length not less than 3 times its breadth, and a sloping floor to assist sludge removal. This is an important maintenance task which must not be neglected. Duplicate tanks built in parallel may also assist regular sludge removal. Sludge may be removed by gravity through a valve at the lowest point in the tank to a sump or directly to treatment. The capacity of a sedimentation tank recommended for temperate climates is of the order of 100 litres per person which gives a retention time of about 12 hrs. In tropical conditions such a long retention time will allow sludge lying on the bottom of the tanks to ferment and rise to the surface to form a scum layer and may also allow some sludge to be carried forward to the next stage of treatment. Experiments in the tropics have shown that most of the action of the sedimentation tank has been completed within 2 hours. This suggests that in the design of tanks for the tropics, having regard to the smaller daily volume of sewage per person likely to be found, a more suitable settlement tank volume should be about 10 to 25 litres per person or less, but desludging should be carried out more often than once daily.

The inlet to a horizontal-flow sedimentation tank should be of the submerged type and the outlet should incorporate a scum board and weir.

A properly designed and maintained sedimentation tank will remove about half the polluting matter from the sewage, and further treatment of the sewage may be carried out in stabilization ponds, by percolating filters or by the activated sludge process.

Anaerobic stabilization ponds (Fig. 30)

There are two kinds of stabilization ponds which make use of two different biological processes. The anaerobic pond uses the same biological process and the same basis for loading as the septic tank and the aqua privy, though on a larger scale, and may be built rather differently. With sewages of normal strength a retention time ($\frac{\text{capacity I}}{\text{flow I/h}}$) of 48 hours is necessary. Anaerobic stabilization ponds should be constructed with watertight linings. Impervious soil is adequate but porous soil will enable leakage to take place for long periods, and solids deposited in anaerobic ponds do not readily seal leakages. The anaerobic process operates in the absence of air so that deep tanks with a small surface area are more efficient than shallow ponds; anaerobic ponds should not be less than 1.5 m deep. Anaerobic stabilization ponds should be filled with water before commissioning. If sewage is admitted to an empty pond offensive conditions will be established which will not be eliminated for many days. Shortly after commissioning with raw sewage, a sludge will accumulate on the bottom of the pond and within about a week a crust will form on the surface which almost eliminates odour. The effluent will be of a similar quality to that of a septic tank or an aqua privy and will require further treatment which may be conveniently carried out in an aerobic stabilization pond, sometimes called an oxidation pond or algal pond. Sludge gradually accumulates in anaerobic ponds; its depth can be measured with a sounding rod and it can be removed when appropriate.

Aerobic stabilization ponds (Fig. 31)

The action of the aerobic stabilization pond is totally different from that of an

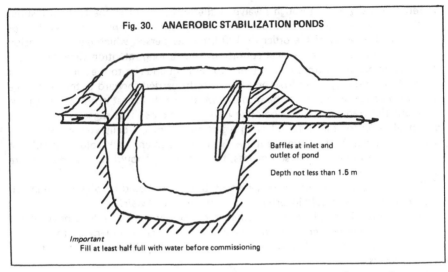

Fig. 30. ANAEROBIC STABILIZATION PONDS

Baffles at inlet and
outlet of pond

Depth not less than 1.5 m

Important
Fill at least half full with water before commissioning

anaerobic pond. In all aerobic biological treatment processes the organic matter causing pollution is consumed by biological organisms requiring oxygen in proportion to the amount of organic matter removed. It is necessary in designing aerobic processes to ensure that the supply of dissolved oxygen is adequate for the loading of organic pollution. In aerobic stabilization ponds oxygen is provided by a growth of algae which depend on photosynthesis. If insufficient oxygen is generated to supply the pollution-consuming organisms, they will not function, and anaerobic organisms will become active and in these circumstances cause offensive odours and polluted effluents to be produced.

The organic pollution of wastes can be measured in a number of ways but for the design of aerobic treatment plants the most useful method is a direct measurement of the amount of oxygen consumed by organisms removing the organic

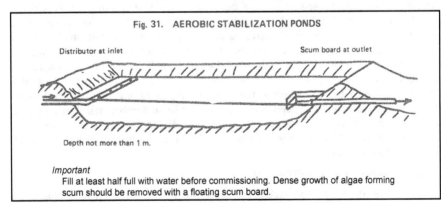

Fig. 31. AEROBIC STABILIZATION PONDS

Distributor at inlet   Scum board at outlet

Depth not more than 1 m.

Important
Fill at least half full with water before commissioning. Dense growth of algae forming scum should be removed with a floating scum board.

matter in the waste in a period of 5 days at 20° C, though the value reached after 3 days at 27° C is more valid in the tropics and usually gives about the same value. This is known as the "biological oxygen demand" or "biochemical oxygen demand" (BOD). BOD may be measured in terms of concentration (mg/litre) in liquid wastes or in quantity (g) in terms of daily demand from a source of waste. Though the test is not difficult to make, it is necessary for a trained laboratory worker to carry it out.

In the absence of such facilities a useful estimate of the biological oxygen demand (BOD) may be made in the following way. Estimates have been made of the BOD value of the excreted wastes of people in different parts of the world. Values vary from 55 g BOD/day in Europe to 36 g BOD/day in parts of India. To this value some allowance must be added for cleansing materials and any other likely additions to the wastes. An acceptable average figure for mixed communities in the tropics would fall between 50 and 60 g BOD per person per day. The strength of the waste, assuming that no industrial pollution is included, may be calculated using the quantity excreted and the volume of water discharged. Thus if the volume of water discharged is 100 litres per person, the concentration of BOD is 500 to 600 mg/litre, or greater or smaller in proportion to the volume of water discharged. This concentration must be reduced to the order of 20 mg/litre before the liquid may be discharged into a watercourse in normal conditions (see chapter 6 for more detail on effluent discharge). Primary treatment in sedimentation tanks may remove about half the BOD, leaving 250-300 mg/litre for treatment. Primary treatment in septic tanks, aqua privies or anaerobic stabilization ponds may remove 70 per cent, leaving 150 to 180 mg/litre at the same rate of water usage. Aqua privies commonly use much less than 100 litres of water per person per day so that stronger pro-rata concentrations must be expected.

When an estimate of the BOD load is finally made, the loading rate on the aerobic stabilization pond can be calculated. As the oxygen supply of the aerobic pond depends largely on algae and sunlight, the working depth of the pond is restricted to 1 m and the loading rate measured in terms of kg BOD per unit area. The amount of sunlight energy that is available per unit area can be measured but it has been found that a close correlation exists between available solar energy and geographical latitude, thus a table of approximate loading rates to produce 80 per cent reduction of BOD can be derived as follows:-

Latitude °N or °S of Equator	BOD load kg/day/100 m²
36	1.5
32	1.75
28	2.0
24	2.25
20	2.5
16	2.75
12	3.0
8 or less	3.25

63

Thus a community of 500 people each with an average water consumption of 100 litres/day per person will discharge 50 000 litres of waste per day containing 25 to 30 kg BOD at a concentration of 500-600 mg/litre. Primary treatment with a 48-h retention anaerobic lagoon of 100,000 litre capacity will reduce the BOD concentration to 150 to 180 mg/litre and the total amount of BOD to 12½ to 15 kg per day. The area of aerobic stabilization pond required to reduce this to 30-36 mg/litre BOD at a latitude of say 10°N will be approximately 400 to 480 m^2.

Aerobic pond systems should always be designed to have at least two ponds in series in order to encourage the separate functions of biological growth, and the physical separation of the treated effluent from the incoming waste. The design of pond systems must also take into consideration the strength of the incoming sewage.

Raw sewage, with less than 250 mg/l BOD can be treated directly in an aerobic pond at the loading rate given for the latitude. A secondary pond with a retention time of about five days should be connected in series.

Where lower water consumption or higher waste discharge produces stronger sewage there is a possibility of local overloading of the primary pond at the loading rates given. Two alternative procedures may be adopted to eliminate this.

Primary treatment by settlement or in an anaerobic pond as in the example given is the best method. The effluent from primary treatment can then be admitted to the primary aerobic pond at the loading rate given for the latitude. This method should always be used with sewage at more than 1000 mg/l BOD. Strong sewage may produce effluents too strong to discharge without additional treatment. In such cases the loading rate on the secondary pond should be calculated from the table and a third pond added with five days retention.

Sewage with BOD in the range 250 to 1000 mg/l can be treated in aerobic ponds without primary treatment if the loading rate is reduced by increasing the area of the first aerobic pond. Areas up to fifty per cent greater than the specified areas may be used but where raw sewage has much in excess of 500 mg/l BOD primary treatment becomes progressively more valuable.

Maintenance in large pond systems can usually be made easier by dividing the total flow between two or more series of ponds operating in parallel.

Single pond systems are likely to form offensive scum on the surface. Aerobic ponds produce profuse growths of algae which should be removed if they clump on the surface and stop sunlight entering the ponds. This may be carried out at suitable intervals by towing a floating scum board down the length of the pond, which should be made long and narrow to facilitate this, and to prevent hydraulic short-circuiting. The effluent from an oxidation pond system will have some green algae present, a BOD value of 50 mg/litre or less and a complete absence of unpleasant smell. Offensive smelling or blackened effluents indicate overloading, requiring extensions to be made to the pond area.

Aerobic ponds should be at least half-filled with water before commissioning to prevent offensive conditions occurring. Many aerobic ponds have been constructed to treat raw sewage. Raw sewage solids float on the surface of these ponds and may also pass out in the effluent. Even if such ponds are not overloaded of-fensive odours often develop. When aerobic ponds are used, some primary treat-ment, either in settling tanks or anaerobic ponds is extremely useful as it may re-move from 50 to 75 per cent of the polluting matter, enabling aerobic ponds to be made smaller.

Important advantages of aerobic ponds are —

a. Cheapness of construction, existing hollows can sometimes be used with slight modifications.
b. Ease of maintenance, little more than gross weed removal, scum removal and bank maintenance is usually required.
c. No power supply is necessary.
d. No mechanical equipment is necessary.
e. The long retention periods in aerobic ponds gives good protection from oc-casional overloading, and removal of pathogens is exceptionally high, often exceeding 95 per cent.
f. BOD loading rates lower than those specified can produce better quality ef-fluents, up to 97 per cent removal can be achieved in multiple pond systems.
g. The algae produced in aerobic ponds can be used as a valuable source of food by many types of fish such as Tilapia, which can be deliberately farmed in final ponds.

Percolating filters (Fig. 32)

Percolating filters are an alternative to aerobic ponds which take up less space though they cost more to construct. In principle the organic pollution in wastes treated on percolating filters is consumed by organisms growing in a thin film on the entire surface of the rock or gravel medium filling the filters. The oxygen they require is obtained by direct diffusion from the air into the thin biological film by the natural ventilation of the filter. The oxygen diffusion capacity of percolating filters is limited by the quantity and specific surface area of the medium provided so that the loading rate on percolating filters is measured in terms of g BOD per m^3 of medium. To remove 90 per cent or more of the BOD the loading rate should not exceed 100 g BOD/m^3 daily. The medium used should be gravel or a durable broken rock graded to 5 to 8 cm grade and free from fine material or dust which may cause blockages. The depth of medium should be not less than 1.2 m, preferably up to 2 m. Under the medium there should be an adequate system of under-drains to enable effluent to leave and air to enter.

Sewage, after settlement, is dosed on the surface of the filters by a mechanical distributor. It is essential that this part of the process is properly carried out; if parts of the filter are not dosed with sewage they cannot contribute any treatment, similarly if the flow is not sufficient to maintain adequate wetting, and the interval of dosing is markedly greater than 15 minutes during periods of normal daytime flow, the organisms will not function efficiently. For these reasons percolating filters are not suitable for the treatment of very strong wastes without some special

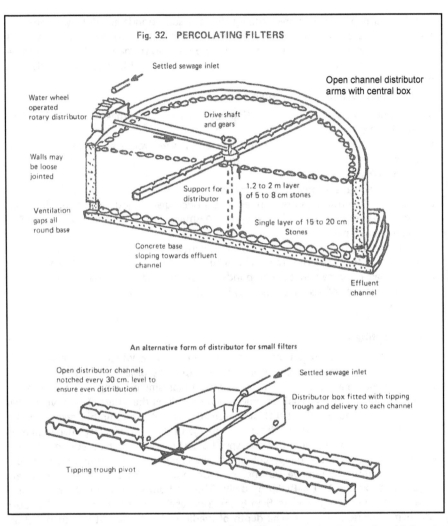

Fig. 32. PERCOLATING FILTERS

Settled sewage inlet

Open channel distributor
arms with central box

Water wheel
operated
rotary distributor

Drive shaft
and gears

Walls may
be loose
jointed

Support for
distributor

1.2 to 2 m layer
of 5 to 8 cm stones

Ventilation
gaps all
round base

Single layer of 15 to 20 cm
Stones

Concrete base
sloping towards effluent
channel

Effluent
channel

An alternative form of distributor for small filters

Open distributor channels
notched every 30 cm. level to
ensure even distribution

Settled sewage inlet

Distributor box fitted with tipping
trough and delivery to each channel

Tipping trough pivot

modification, such as recirculation of the effluent, or the use of a high-rate preliminary filter in a two-stage plant. Efficient distributors can be improvised for small filters but for larger installation it is preferable to install manufactured distributors. These usually have rotating arms powered by the sewage flow.

Percolating filters may operate on a fill-and-draw principle operated entirely by siphon action which enables the medium to be flooded and drained at intervals of not greater than 12 hours. The medium used is 1 cm grade or smaller in beds not more than 60 cm deep. Hydraulic loading rates of settled sewage or septic tank effluent may be 0.5 to 0.1 m ^{3} per m^2 per day. Optimum rates of flooding

66

and draining are about once per hour. It is very important that filters of this type are not dosed with sewage containing gross suspended matter.

Much of the action of a percolating filter, in removing organic pollution from the sewage, results in the formation of surplus bacterial film which is washed out in the effluent, and must be removed in a final sedimentation tank before effluent is discharged. The design of the final sedimentation tank or humus tank can be the same as that of the primary sedimentation tank but no screens are necessary.

Fly larvae perform important functions in percolating filters. Adult flies rarely stray more than a few metres from percolating filters. In some parts of the tropics lizards are able to inhabit the surface of filters and emerging flies are almost eliminated. In other regions fly populations have been observed sufficiently dense and able to fly far enough to create a local nuisance although their maximum range is seldom more than two or three hundred metres. If filters are sited downwards of the prevailing wind and at a reasonable distance from habitations any potential fly nuisance can be avoided.

Trade waste disposal

Many trade waste waters are being produced in parts of the tropics where no proper disposal facilities exist. Many, such as coffee waste, cotton processing waste, tannery waste, sisal waste, slaughterhouse waste, are of a highly polluting character, and should not be discharged untreated to waters likely to be used as sources of domestic supply unless the dilution is extremely high and there is an adequate delay period before water is abstracted. Most of these wastes can be treated by similar processes to those used for domestic wastes provided care is taken to control pH value within the range 6.0 to 8.5, to exclude toxic substances and ensure that an adequate supply of nutrients is present. The latter requirement may often be satisfied by treating trade waste liquors mixed with domestic sewage. Sedimentation and chemical flocculation may be used and most biological treatment processes may be used if the BOD loading is suitably adjusted. Expert advice should be consulted if trade wastes are to be treated.

A simple method of testing sewage effluents

The proper tests for sewage effluents should be carried out in a well equipped laboratory but the following simple test will indicate whether a process is giving adequate treatment.

A sample of the effluent is transferred to a small bottle which must be completely filled with as little aeration as possible, then stoppered and put in a dark place at a temperature of $27^\circ C$. Ambient temperatures in the tropics are sufficiently high not to seriously influence the test. The incubated sample should be smelled from time to time. Initially there should be no characteristic smell of hydrogen sulphide, H_2S (like bad eggs). If the effluent contains polluting matter this will gradually be consumed by bacteria which will use up the dissolved oxygen in the liquid. After the dissolved oxygen is completely consumed the bacteria will break down dissolved nitrates, and when that source of oxygen is exhausted they will break down sulphates liberating hydrogen sulphide which can be detected by smell If this last stage is reached in less than three days the effluent is said to be unstable and requires further purification. The test may be made more sensitive by adding a blue dye (methylene blue) to the effluent, using a concentrated stock solution to make a concentration of 1.33 mg/l in the sample. The consumption of oxygen affects the colour of the dye so that if no blue remains after three days the effluent is said to be unstable and requires further purification. This test cannot be used directly on anaerobic effluents.

All sewage treatment processes need time to mature so that tests carried out in the first two or three months after commissioning a treatment process should be interpreted accordingly.

All methods of sewage disposal which do not remove the pollution from the community must be sited with great care to prevent a direct health hazard and to prevent any danger of pollution of the water source or the supply to some nearby community. These two points cannot be too strongly stressed and must be carefully examined by an advisor setting up a water supply and disposal system.

Selecting sewage treatment systems to suit local conditions

Observations of local conditions coupled with a reasonable estimate of future development will indicate the extent to which communities can be served by pipe lines. A single collection point can make use of larger scale treatment plant but very scattered communities may be best served by being connected in groups to a number of small treatment plants. If the density of population increases small treatment plants of a simple nature can be closed and groups connected together making maximum use of the small feeder sewers. When a treatment site has been chosen at a reasonable distance from housing and water sources the next step is to estimate the probable pollution load. If partial measurement is possible the results can be extrapolated to include the whole population. If no measurement are possible the method given in the section on aerobic stabilization ponds may be used. The BOD contribution suggested for each person is a deliberately high figure where no actual analytical measurements are made. This provides a safety factor wich allows for bulky cleansing materials, and unexpected or temporary increases in population. Most sewage treatment plant operate well if underloaded to some extent . Overloading has more serious consequences particularly to some aerobic processes. If BOD measurements are made and individual contributions calculated to be much less than 30 gm per adult per day it is possible that not all wastes are being collected in the sewerage system. Irregularities should be investigated to ensure that they do not constitute a danger to health. Any trade waste which may be intermittent and sometimes on a very small scale such as brewing or tanning, should be separately estimated and due allowance made in the total volume and strength of sewage to be treated.

It is then necessary to decide the quality of effluent that can be discharged

68

Small volumes of effluent discharged to large perennial rivers in areas where water abstraction points are not affected, do not always need a high degree of purification. The simplest systems for partial treatment are primary sedimentation tanks or lagoons, and anaerobic ponds or septic tanks. These are able to remove from 50 to 75 per cent of polluting matter and even more suspended matter.

If secondary treatment is necessary, the first choice in tropical areas could be aerobic pond systems. If site conditions such as insufficient available area, steep sloping sites or unstable or very permeable soil are unfavourable to the choice of aerobic pond systems the most suitable alternative is some form of percolating filter making use of local rock. Costs of percolating filters and mechanical distributors should be compared with the extra costs of land required for aerobic ponds and extra costs of sewerage that may be required in order to utilize an alternative site.

Where any form of secondary treatment is used the plant should be made large enough to treat the expected volume and strength of sewage, and provision should be made to deal with storm water that may be included in the flow, and an increased load that may be expected as local development expands. Secondary processes that are not overloaded can be operated to produce final effluent fit for discharge to most rivers if water abstraction does not take place too close to the point of discharge. Effluents can also be used for crop irrigation, but for most edible crops high quality effluents may be required. Tertiary treatment by grass plots or lagoons fulfills most of the requirements but chlorination is sometimes specified and may be installed using equipment similar to that described for the chlorination of water supplies. The chlorine demand of sewage effluents can be very much higher than that found in most raw waters and it is lowest in effluents that have been given most treatment. Well operated primary, secondary and tertiary treatment systems are still advisable even when chlorination is used in irrigation schemes.

Chlorine is a powerful bactericide and it has the same effect on beneficial water-borne organisms. Although sewage effluents can be effectively disinfected using chlorine this effect should be employed with some care. If effluents are discharged to streams with the intermittent seasonal flows that are common in semi-arid areas, there will be periods when the whole flow of the stream consists of treated effluent. If this has been disinfected with chlorine all of the beneficial organisms in the stream will also be lost, and a valuable contribution of quality improvement from the normal stream environment will be lost. The dangers of each course of action have to be carefully considered in this difficult type of situation.

Chapter Six

Final Water and Sludge Disposal

After waste waters have been treated their final disposal must be considered. Direct discharge to a watercourse may be possible if the dilution is adequate, 9 times or more for good quality effluents, or if the watercourse is not used as a source of drinking water supply, less dilution can be employed. Very small discharges can be safely disposed of in soakaways. Discharges of larger volume, if not of adequate quality after secondary treatment, may need tertiary treatment if the dilution capacity of the receiving water is too low. The sludges produced in sewage treatment processes must also be disposed of with proper care.

Soakaways (Fig. 33)

These may be in the form of pits or loose-jointed subsurface drains, and if of adequate size and sited at a safe distance from water sources are a useful method of disposal for the discharges of many types of aqua privy or septic tank installation. They should be constructed in permeable soils only and no single pit or drain should deal with more than 5000 litres of effluent per day. A simple test for permeability can be made by digging a pit approximately 1 m diameter and 2 m deep. The pit should be filled with clean water. All water should seep away within 24 hours in suitable soil. The volume of the pits should be not less than the daily discharge. Pits may be lined with broken rock, open-jointed brick or concrete blocks. Between the lining and the soil surface a layer of broken rock 15 cm thick should be packed. The wall from ground level to the level of the inlet pipe should be sealed with cement, and a strong cover provided. An alternative method of construction dispenses with the lining below the level of the inlet pipe; instead the whole pit is filled with broken rock about 10 cm grade or larger. The inlet pipe should be installed to discharge in the centre of the pit.

Drainage trenches may be constructed in permeable soil by digging trenches 1 m deep and 0.5 m wide with a gradient of 1 in 30. Crushed rock or gravel 5 to 10 cm grade is placed in the trench to a depth of 0.5 m, a few cm of gravel about 2 to 3 cm is placed on top of the coarse material, then soil can be replaced if care is taken not to allow the soil to clog the gravel. A strip of plastic film laid above the gravel before the soil is returned reduces the likelihood of clogging. The length of trench required is about 1.0 to 1.5 m per person depending upon the permeability of the soil.

Fig. 33. SOAKAWAYS AND SOIL DRAINS

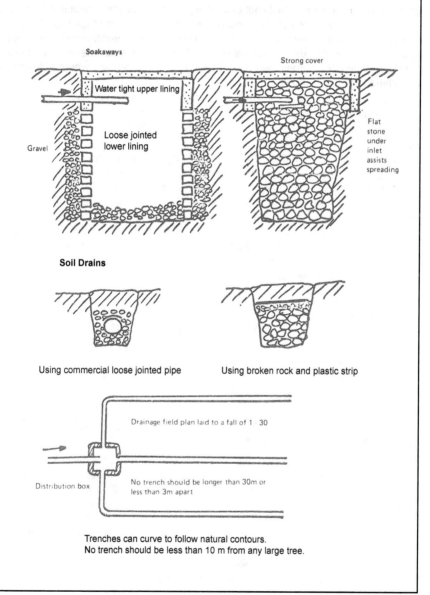

Soakaways

Strong cover

Water tight upper lining

Gravel

Loose jointed
lower lining

Flat
stone
under
inlet
assists
spreading

Soil Drains

Using commercial loose jointed pipe   Using broken rock and plastic strip

Drainage field plan laid to a fall of 1 : 30

Distribution box   No trench should be longer than 30m or
less than 3m apart

Trenches can curve to follow natural contours.
No trench should be less than 10 m from any large tree.

71

Tertiary treatment of effluents

The aim of sewage-treatment processes is to produce an effluent suitable for discharge into receiving water. If the maximum tolerable additional pollution load in the receiving water is considered to be a BOD of 2 mg/litre at the point of discharge then the effluent should have a BOD not exceeding 20 mg/litre if the minimum dilution factor is 1 volume to 9 volumes of receiving water. This standard of effluent quality is often relaxed in the tropics where rivers can be extremely large, enabling very high dilutions to be made, or where discharges can be made to swamps or other receiving waters, not likely to be used immediately as a drinking water supply, and where effluents may be retained for long periods.

If the secondary treatment processes such as stabilization ponds, percolating filters or activated sludge plants do not meet with required quality of effluent this may be caused by incorrect design, incorrect operation or overloading. It may not be possible to alter the fundamental design of a sewage-treatment plant without building extensions. Incorrect operation can be put right if a critical examination of the works is made and training and advice supplied where necessary. Overloading may require extensions to be made to the plant. If the quality of the effluent is, however, not grossly lower than that required for safe discharge a tertiary treatment stage may be added to the process. The main purpose of most tertiary treatment processes is the reduction of the concentration of suspended matter in the effluents with a consequent reduction in BOD value and also often a considerable reduction in the numbers of bacteria discharged. Three methods of tertiary treatment are appropriate to rural areas in the tropics. They are compared in the following table.

	Area loading rate $(m^3/m^2 d)$	Per cent reduction of		
		SS	BOD	E.coli
Lagoons	0.5	40	40	70
Banks' clarifiers	24.0	50	30	25
Grass plots	0.85	70	50	90

Lagoons for tertiary treatment of effluents

Tertiary treatment lagoons are simple to construct if sufficient land is available. Their action is similar to that of a sedimentation tank of very large capacity. In tropical conditions algae may flourish in shallow lagoons in depths up to 1 m, so that a minimum depth of about 2 m should be available at least in the region of the point of discharge. If aerobic stabilization pond effluent is being treated it may contain high concentrations of motile algae so that particular attention should be paid to avoiding short-circuiting of flow and to maintaining adequate depth of liquid (over 2 m) throughout the lagoon to discourage further algae growth. The discharge from lagoons should be taken from the middle level between bottom and surface. Suspended matter accumulates in lagoons but if depths are adequate it seldom proves offensive. Mosquito breeding is a risk in lagoons but routine oil or insecticide treatment and maintenance of the banks can control this problem. It is often possible to establish fish in tertiary treatment lagoons, which serve as a useful indication of effluent quality and may also provide a measure of mosquito larvae control. A suitable loading rate on lagoons is about 0.5 m^3/m^2 daily.

Banks' clarifiers

The Banks' clarifier is the most compact tertiary treatment process recommended though the quality of effluent is still markedly improved. The Banks' clarifier is essentially an upward-flow filter containing a bed of gravel, 1 to 1½ cm grade, about 15 cm thick, supported on a perforated base which can be suspended in the top of a sedimentation tank in the manner shown in Fig. 34. Alternatively it may be built as a separate structure like an upward-flow sand filter with a layer of clarified effluent not less than 30 cm deep above the gravel layer. Solids accumulate within, and on the upper surface of the gravel layer. When the upper surface is seen to be uniformly covered, or when the suspended-solids concentration in the final effluent substantially rises, the bed should be cleaned. This may be accomplished by lowering the liquid level in the humus tank, as would occur when sludge is being removed. If more vigorous cleaning proves to be necessary, a jet of final effluent from a hose during the level-lowering operation should suffice; raking the gravel is seldom necessary though may be needed to clean a neglected filter. A suitable loading rate on Banks' clarifier is about 24 m^3/m^2 daily.

Grass plots (Fig. 35)

Grass plots are possibly the simplest effluent tertiary treatment device to construct, and it can be seen from the table that correctly loaded they will accomplish the highest rate of removal of BOD, suspended solids and E. coli, common intestinal bacteria. Plots should be reasonably even and sloped towards the collection channels at a gradient of about 1 in 50. The operation of grass plots depends on the horizontal flow of effluent passing through the mesh of the grass blades which filter out solids and provide a well aerated environment. In tropical conditions evaporation may at times be sufficient to prevent any final effluent remaining for discharge. Some effluent will percolate into porous ground so that the possibility of contaminating ground water, though small, should be considered. No special seeding needs to be done, coarse natural grass is satisfactory. During the operation of the plot grass will grow rapidly and solids will accumulate so that it is necessary to divide the plot into a series of areas which can be disconnected in turn and allowed to dry. The surplus grass can then be removed. Cuttings should not be allowed to remain on the area owing to the danger of further pollution as they decompose. Solids need not be removed until they physically impede flow, which may not be necessary for a number of years. A suitable loading rate on grass plots is about 0.85 m^3/m^2 daily.

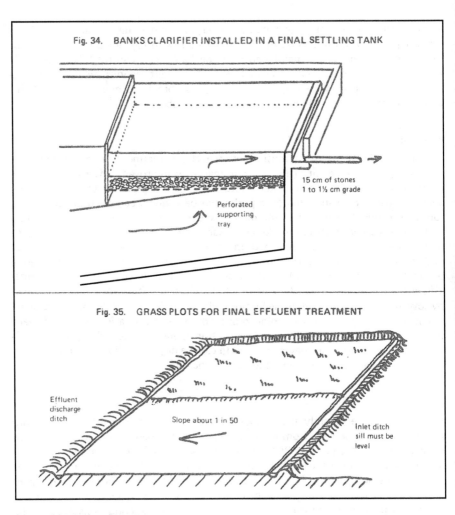

Fig. 34. BANKS CLARIFIER INSTALLED IN A FINAL SETTLING TANK

15 cm of stones
1 to 1½ cm grade

Perforated
supporting
tray

Fig. 35. GRASS PLOTS FOR FINAL EFFLUENT TREATMENT

Effluent
discharge
ditch

Slope about 1 in 50

Inlet ditch
sill must be
level

Anaerobic sludge digestion

The processes of sewage purification produce quantities of sludge which must be removed at regular intervals from settling tanks and humus tanks and less frequently from septic tanks, aquaprivies and anaerobic lagoons. Much of this sludge may be dried without further treatment but it is desirable that sludge from primary settling tanks should be subjected to a period of further treatment to reduce the risks of disease transmission and to render the sludge less offensive.

A useful process for this purpose is anaerobic digestion in which many of the functions of the anaerobic stabilization pond occur but on a more intensive scale. The main objectives of anaerobic digestion are the reduction of the quantity of sludge for final disposal and the reduction of pathogenic organisms and offensive smells. The anaerobic decomposition of organic matter also liberates carbon dioxide and methane gas which can be collected from suitably designed digesters and used as a fuel gas. The final digested sludge has almost no smell, can be easily dried or applied to agricultural land as a source of humus with some associated fertilizer value. The fertilizer value of digested sludge is not high and may not be consistent. Sludge derived from the treatment of a mixture of domestic waste and certain industrial wastes may contain metallic salts in concentrations harmful both to the digestion process and subsequently to crops, but this situation is extremely unlikely in rural areas.

Anaerobic digestion is most efficient at about 30-35°C but at temperatures below about 10°C reactions are very slow. Average ambient temperatures in most tropical regions are high enough to enable digesters to function well without extra heating. On a small community scale where sludge production and potential gas consumption are too small to justify the extra expense and care needed to ensure a reliable gas supply, simple batch type digester pits are convenient and easy to manage. Watertight pits not less than 2 metres deep and preferably up to 4 metres deep can be equipped with a loading pipe to enable liquid sludge to be admitted to the bottom throughout the charging period. A layer of dried grass or soil scattered on the surface to encourage the rapid formation of a dry crust will seal the contents to maintain anaerobic conditions and reduce any offensive smells that may develop in the early stages of digestion. The necessary storage capacity can be calculated assuming a total output of primary and secondary sludge equivalent to about 1 to 2 litres per person per day. The time required for digestion varies mainly with ambient temperature but minimum retention period allowed should be from 3 months at 25°C or over, to 12 months at 15°C. After the pit is filled the loading pipe can be removed and the surface of the sludge capped with more soil and securely fenced to prevent accidents. A second digester can be filled while the first is digesting though it is usually more convenient to operate a group of 3 or 4 pits. At the end of the digestion period the bulk of the sludge can be removed and spread on land or dried for further storage, leaving a few cm of digested sludge in the pit to seed the next charge.

If it is considered desirable to use anaerobic digestion as a source of methane gas, sewage sludges can be treated in combination with animal wastes, many types of vegetable waste and garbage. The total output of digestible waste from an average family is not sufficient to generate enough gas to maintain a domestic supply, and if this is required supplementary wastes must be incorporated. On large installations the sludge produced by a community such as a residential school might produce enough gas to heat water or to perform some other simple central function.

Digester gas is usually about 65 per cent methane and 30 per cent carbon dioxide plus traces of other gases. If the digesting wastes contain significant concentration of sulphates some H_2S may be formed. As a fuel, digester gas is equivalent to rather more than its own volume of coal gas but about 1500 to 2000 litres are required to do the same duty as 1 litre of paraffin, petrol or diesel oil. Storage of gas on a large scale is therefore an important requirement and since the gas is highly inflammable and able to form explosive mixtures with air, the safety of gas generation and storage is of great importance and should be under the direct supervision of a responsible and trained attendant.

The minimum worthwhile size of a gas generating digester is about 4 m³ capacity with a gas holder of not less than 2 m³ capacity though much larger sizes are more usual. The gas production from a continuously fed digester with a mean retention time of 90 days at 20-25°C is about 0.5 m³ per day per m³ of digester capacity. Temperatures up to 35°C enable the rate of gas production to be increased by a factor up to about 6 times, and retention times at higher temperatures can be made shorter but much depends on the type of organic matter used.

To start a digester functioning, a seed of septic tank sludge or mature anaerobic lagoon sludge should be mixed with diluted primary or humus sludge. After a period of 2 or 3 weeks the maintainance of the digester lies mainly in regulating the input of sludge, the discharge of final sludge where necessary, and attention to safety precautions. The pH value in the digester should be tested from time to time, the desired range is from 6.8 to 7.5. If the pH value rises above 7.5, usually when fresh sludge is added, the carbon dioxide formed will gradually correct this. If the pH value falls below 6.8 this should be corrected by adding a small quantity of lime to

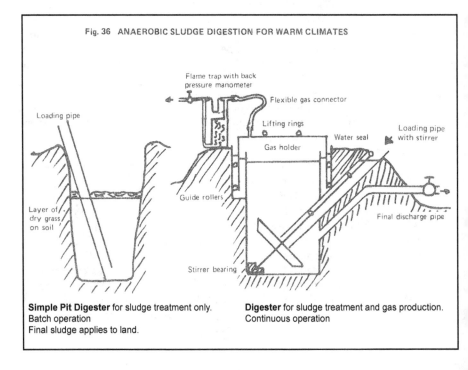

Fig. 36 ANAEROBIC SLUDGE DIGESTION FOR WARM CLIMATES

Flame trap with back pressure manometer

Flexible gas connector

Loading pipe

Lifting rings

Loading pipe with stirrer

Water seal

Gas holder

Guide rollers

Layer of dry grass on soil

Final discharge pipe

Stirrer bearing

Simple Pit Digester for sludge treatment only.
Batch operation
Final sludge applies to land.

Digester for sludge treatment and gas production.
Continuous operation

raise the pH and maintain healthy biological activity. If the retention time allowed is adequate for the prevailing temperature the final sludge has little smell and very few surviving pathogenic organisms. The organic carbon concentration is reduced but the nitrogen in the sludge remains, mainly in the form of ammonia. This increases the value of sludge applied directly to land where it should be allowed to remain undisturbed for a period of about a week before cattle or other stock are admitted. The liquid in the digested sludge is still very polluting in character and should not be allowed to drain directly to a watercourse without further treatment.

The two main types of digesters are shown in fig. 36 though many variations are possible. Continuous digesters can be fitted with heaters to maintain digester temperatures and mixing devices to improve efficiency and reduce the likelihood of scum formation. If gas collection is not considered necessary, digesters may be operated in the tropics with retention times as low as 30 days. To simplify operation at short retention times the raw sludge should be thin enough to be considered a liquid. Most primary settlement and humus tank sludges are suitable if tanks are regularly desludged and no consolidation is allowed to take place. Septic tank and aqua privy sludges are often consolidated and too thick for simple digestion. Dilution with sewage to a reasonably liquid state is usually sufficient. Most animal wastes also require dilution in the same way.

Although it is possible to couple latrines directly to anaerobic digesters, the cost of such a system is higher than that for most other latrine systems and the output of gas is not usually very high.

If used for lighting and cooking only, the average family requires about 200 litres or more of gas per day. Water heating and room heating consume very much more gas. The potential daily gas production assuming that all excreta are collected and treated is as follows.

	litres/day
Adult humans	15-25
Pigs	50-100
Cows	300-600
Sheep/goats	20-40
Chickens	2-4

Anaerobic digestion for gas production should be considered as a process most suitable for operation by a responsible attendant on the largest scale possible either at a sewage works or possibly a farm where large amounts of animal excreta are regularly available. Anaerobic digestion is of great value in reducing potential health risks in most kinds of sewage sludge and makes the potential fertilizer value more readily and more safely available for farm use. The collection and utilization of the gas is essentially a large scale operation with a need for great emphasis on safety. If the standard of technology available is not high enough to ensure safety in the operation of the gas supply it is better to use digesters for sludge treatment only and allow gas to be wasted to the atmosphere.

Composting (Fig. 37)

Sewage sludge may be safely disposed of together with domestic refuse and animal and vegetable waste by composting, which is a process very suitable to rural areas where the supply of compost is of positive value. It is possible to couple the latrine directly to the composting process but the periodic attention which must be paid to composting and the increased risk of fly breeding detracts from the convenience of the latrine. Composting is most usefully organized on a centralized basis utilizing sludge from sewage treatment, night soil, and domestic refuse which can be collected on a scale of about 1 m³ per day for every 500 persons served. Grass cuttings and other agricultural wastes may also be used.

Composting may be carried out in pits which confine the raw material safely but require more capital outlay and more manual labour than composting carried out in stacks, which are cheaper and more flexible with regard to capacity. Stacks may be built on areas of fairly level ground with sufficient slope to enable surface run-off to be collected in ditches and soakaways. A minimum effective size of stack is about 2 m wide at the base and any convenient length. It can be started by placing a 15 cm layer of coarse vegetable refuse on the ground and adding a 15 cm layer of domestic refuse free from glass, tins and plastic waste on top, and a depression formed in the middle to allow about 5 cm of sludge to be added. Sufficient space should be left at the sides to retain all sludge in the stack. The sludge should then be covered immediately with about 20 to 30 cm of refuse which may be mixed with waste vegetable matter or straw. Alternate layers of sludge and refuse can be added to a maximum height of about 1½ m in progressively smaller layers to allow sloping sides to be formed on which no sludge should be visible.

Composting is an aerobic process for which some moisture is necessary so that periodic turning is needed, and it may also become necessary to water the partially composted material in prolonged periods of dry weather to maintain about 60% moisture content. Sewage effluent can be conveniently used for this purpose. After about a week the compost is turned manually or by machine so that the top layers of the original heap become the bottom layers of the new heap. If the volume is substantially reduced a fresh layer of sludge topped with domestic refuse or vegetable matter may be added and water added if necessary. The whole stack should be turned a second time in about another week; by this time there should be little visible evidence of the raw sludge. If no sludge was added at the first turn it is unlikely that a third turn will be needed. The stack should be allowed to stand for about a further 2 to 6 weeks during which little more than watering will be necessary. The turning process tends to eliminate fly breeding so that if excessive fly breeding occurs a further turn may be necessary.

During the process of composting temperatures of 55° to 70°C are generated in the centre of the stack, which in the period of composting effectively destroy most of the pathogenic bacteria, parasites, eggs and fly larvae which may be present.

Some experiment is advisable to find the most suitable proportions of domestic refuse and grass cuttings to be added, and also to maintain the most suitable moisture content in relation to prevailing weather conditions. The final product

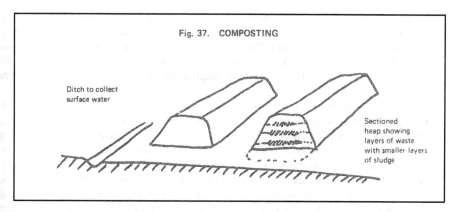

Fig. 37. COMPOSTING

Ditch to collect
surface water

Sectioned
heap showing
layers of waste
with smaller layers
of sludge

of a well-run compost heap should be dark in colour, friable, contain very little visible uncomposted material, and be free from offensive odours and from almost all pathogenic organisms. The manurial value of compost depends very much on the nature of the raw material, but is always sufficient to be of value in small-scale gardening or farming operations.

Final sludge dewatering (Fig. 38)

The most suitable method of dewatering sludge in the tropics is by exposure on open drying beds. These may be areas of land graded to about 1 in 200 enclosed by low walls. The floors of large drying beds should be equipped with a drainage system and covered to a depth of about 20 cm with gravel or broken rock graded from 4 cm at the bottom to about 2.8 cm at the top, then finally covered with a level layer of 5 cm of 1½-3 mm coarse sand. Sludge is admitted to the drying bed in

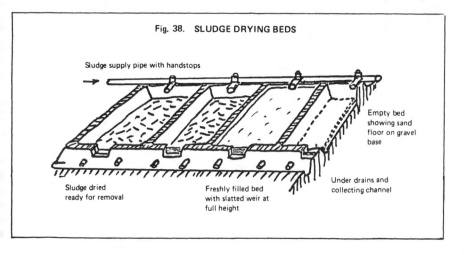

Fig. 38. SLUDGE DRYING BEDS

Sludge supply pipe with handstops

Empty bed
showing sand
floor on gravel
base

Under drains and
collecting channel

Sludge dried
ready for removal

Freshly filled bed
with slatted weir at
full height

layers not more than 20 cm deep. After 24 hours the sludge will have separate to form a thickened lower layer and an upper layer of relatively clear liquid whic may be decanted over a suitable weir which may be constructed from woode slats. The supernatant liquid is usually heavily polluted and should not be di charged to receiving water; it may be discharged to soak pits or returned to th treatment process.

In most tropical conditions the remaining layer of sludge will dry to a spadeabl consistency in a week or less, when it can be removed and stacked for a perioc which encourages further biological action, before application to agricultur land. If heavy rains prevent drying, sludge may be stored in open tanks to underg further anaerobic decomposition before eventual transfer to the drying beds. I temperate climates the usual allocation of drying beds is on a scale of about 1 m for every 2 persons. The more rapid rate of drying in the tropics will allow high loadings up to 1 m^2 for every 10 persons. Single drying beds do not allow sufficier intermittent operation to permit removal of dried sludge; not less than three an preferably more than four drying beds are more convenient to manage. Drying bec may be built in a variety of sizes, and in small installations the provision of pipe underdrains is not absolutely necessary.

Owing to the high risk of parasites such as hookworm surviving in raw sewag sludge in tropical areas, the direct application of raw sludge to drying beds is i advisable. Raw sludge should receive some preliminary treatment such as digestio before application to drying beds.

Liquid digested sludge has a worthwhile fertilizer value but should be applie to land with some care. Quantities produced are likely to be about 1½ litres pe person per day. If digested sludge is applied directly to agricultural land care shoul be taken to avoid heavy accumulation of sludge in one place. In general a secon application should not be made until the first application has dried and show some sign of absorption.

Chapter Seven

Temporary and Emergency Treatment

All emergency treatment may be considered as temporary, though temporary treatment need not be treated as an emergency. The scale of temporary treatment systems may range from the scale appropriate to moving camps of the smallest size to the size of large military units. Emergency treatment systems may also vary in scale but situations periodically occur in the tropics where emergency treatment must be organised for many hundreds of thousands of people in desperate circumstances.

The smallest scale will be considered first. As much good quality water should be carried as may be appropriate for short journeys. For longer journeys where water supplies must be picked up en route the only likely sources are surface sources. Care should be exercised to avoid as far as possible obvious pollution from animal and human sources. Cloudy or muddy water should be strained through one or more layers of clean cotton cloth such as that commonly marketed as amerikani. Sterilization can then be carried out by boiling for about 20 minutes. Chlorine tablets can be obtained and used according to the maker's directions. As a result of this treatment safe water can be produced. If the taste is objectionable the inclusion of a few pieces of charcoal when boiling may improve this.

Emergencies occur at times in the most well organized safaris. Mechanised transport can break-down in dry country. The main problem then becomes one of finding a source of water. In extreme circumstances drinkable water can be found in many plants, and in addition the blood and body fluids of animals and birds can be used. At the last resort it is a mistake to hoard water, as dehydration of the body goes on the whole time and unless the body's water losses are made up, exhaustion quickly sets in. The rate of body dehydration at a range of temperatures can be seen from the table on page 82.

Sanitation in the smallest temporary camps needs to be no more than shallow pit latrines which may be equipped with any sort of toilet and shelter which may be appropriate. Proper care should be taken, however, by correct siting, to avoid polluting water sources at all times.

Large temporary camps may adopt the same methods of treatment scaled up accordingly. Chlorination is a more suitable water sterilizing method than boiling for large camps and may be carried out in portable canvas or plastic tanks in a batch process, by a person made responsible for water supply, who should if possible

Expected survival time in shade with limited water stock
Survival time days

Maximum shade temp.	With no water (days)	Total water stock (l) per person 1	2	4	10	20
°F °C						
120 50	2	2	2	2.5	3	4.5
110 44	3	3	3.5	4.0	5	7
100 38	5	5.5	6	7	8.5	13.5
90 32	7	8	9	10.5	15	23
80 26	9	10	11	13	19	29
70 20	10	11	12	14	20.5	32

carry the equipment for measuring residual chlorine concentration. On a large scale, filtration through cloth may be greatly improved by dosing the raw water with alum in a batch process. An average dose of about 60 mg/litre may be applied in the form of a strong solution. In soft acid waters, such as swamp waters, a little lime may also be required. If an obvious flocculant precipitate has not formed within 15 minutes of mixing the alum solution with the main body of water, a larger dose should be tried. The flocculated water may then be allowed to settle for from 4 to 6 hours and the clarified supernatant liquid can be siphoned or filtered into the chlorinating tank. Up to 90 per cent of the water will be available for chlorination (Fig. 39).

On the largest scale, temporary and emergency treatment is required for the large camps set up for refugees from natural and other disasters. Many of the problems that afflict such camps are a function of their size. The organizers of large refugee camps can take many relevant leaves from books on military hygiene and field engineering. In order to make organization possible, refugees should be grouped in units of not more than 2000. Each group can have persons appointed and trained to be responsible for food, water, sanitation and all the other domestic necessities within its allocated area. Units of this nature can be grouped together in camps of much larger size if necessary.

The selection of a suitable site can make the organization of public health matters easier. A sloping site with good surface drainage which can be improved by trenching should be selected, not too close to the water source, so that surface drainage can be diverted to the downstream side of the water abstraction site. Close proximity to towns should be avoided. Water can be abstracted from the most suitable source and treated by flocculation, sedimentation and subsequent chlorination. Indiscriminate use of untreated water should be prevented. Sanitation must be provided on a communal basis. For large-scale emergency facilities black polythene film has many uses, as well as being light, cheap, and easy to transport by air. A form of aqua privy combined with an oxidation pond may be

(Continued on p. 85).

Fig. 39. WATER TREATMENT FOR EMERGENCIES

Emergency storage tanks

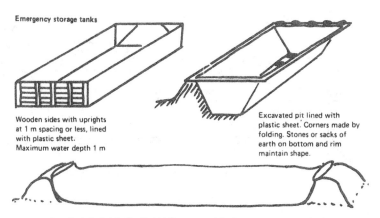

Wooden sides with uprights
at 1 m spacing or less, lined
with plastic sheet.
Maximum water depth 1 m

Excavated pit lined with
plastic sheet. Corners made by
folding. Stones or sacks of
earth on bottom and rim
maintain shape.

Length of plastic tube (lay flat) laid between earth banks to support upturned ends.

Cloth filter

Wooden frame supporting 2 or 3 layers of
cloth without joints or seams.
Removes suspended matter only.

Emergency supply layout

Primary tank for storage
settlement and coagulation

Secondary tank for filtration
chlorination and storage—
cloth filters 1 in use 1 spare

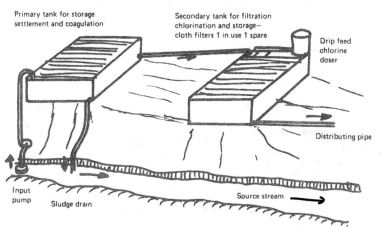

Drip feed
chlorine
doser

Distributing pipe

Input
pump

Sludge drain

Source stream

All tanks should be covered. Plastic sheet will suffice.

83

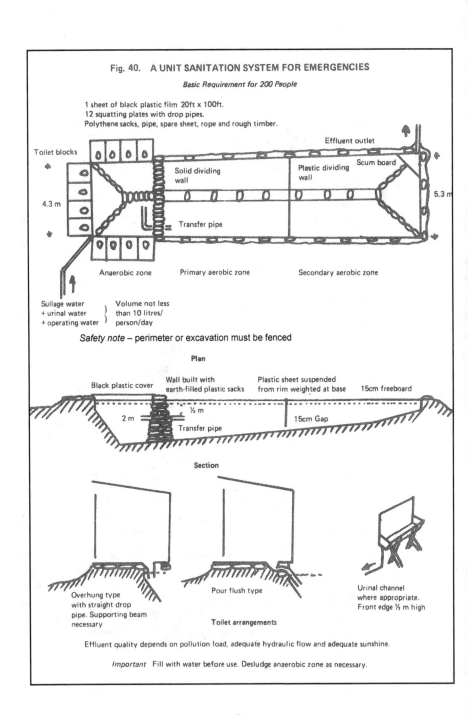

Fig. 40. A UNIT SANITATION SYSTEM FOR EMERGENCIES

Basic Requirement for 200 People

1 sheet of black plastic film 20ft x 100ft.
12 squatting plates with drop pipes.
Polythene sacks, pipe, spare sheet, rope and rough timber.

Toilet blocks

Effluent outlet

Solid dividing wall

Plastic dividing wall

Scum board

4.3 m

5.3 m

Transfer pipe

Anaerobic zone   Primary aerobic zone   Secondary aerobic zone

Sullage water
+ urinal water   } Volume not less
+ operating water   than 10 litres/
person/day

Safety note – perimeter or excavation must be fenced

Plan

Black plastic cover   Wall built with   Plastic sheet suspended
earth-filled plastic sacks   from rim weighted at base   15cm freeboard

½ m

2 m   15cm Gap

Transfer pipe

Section

Overhung type
with straight drop
pipe. Supporting beam
necessary

Pour flush type

Urinal channel
where appropriate.
Front edge ½ m high

Toilet arrangements

Effluent quality depends on pollution load, adequate hydraulic flow and adequate sunshine.

Important Fill with water before use. Desludge anaerobic zone as necessary.

84

constructed by digging a lagoon and lining it with polythene film reinforced with polythene bags filled with soil after the fashion of sand bags (Fig. 40). A similar method of building using a mixture of soil reinforced with about 6 per cent of cement developed by P.R. Moody can be used for more permanent structures (*The introduction of rainwater catchment tanks and micro-irrigation to Botswana*, ITDG 1969). A polythene sheet 20ft by 100ft can provide an emergency sewage treatment plant for about 200 people or more. If larger sheets of polythene can be obtained larger facilities can be built but the 200-person single facility has certain advantages and can be multiplied to cope with the necessary population. Treatment plants must be partially filled with water before use (surface water will suffice) and after the plants are functioning the effluents can be combined to some extent with the surface water drainage system, provided the drains are reasonably protected.

The operation of such simple sanitation systems depends on diluting water being added to the raw waste at the rate of about 20 to 25 litres per person per day, to produce an initial concentration of about 1500 mg/litre BOD in the anaerobic compartment. The volume of the anaerobic compartment should be constructed to provide a retention period of not less than 2 days to the total flow. This will enable a clarified effluent containing about 500 mg/litre BOD to pass through the transfer pipe to the primary aerobic zone. The BOD reduction achieved in the aerobic zones can be calculated from the loading rate per unit area, and the latitude. Further aerobic ponds may be added to reduce the BOD to acceptable levels for final discharge. Sludge accumulates rapidly in the anaerobic zone, and to ensure continued functioning surplus sludge must be periodically withdrawn, and stored in plastic storage containers fitted with gas vents. After a period of 3 to 6 months the sludge will be well digested and almost free from harmful organisms, and then may be buried or discharged on land.

Some notes on water supply and sanitation in refugee camps

One of the authors recently worked for some time in a series of refugee camps in the tropics that had been erected on a temporary basis, but circumstances required their continued use for periods of eight months to more than one year. The following observations may be of help to those with similar problems.

1. Water supply

An adequate number of tube wells (hand pumps fitted to small boreholes) were initially provided but in some camps wells ran dry. In many camps, wells gradually blocked at the screens due to deposits of soil and deposits of precipitated iron salts. Most of the ground water in the area had concentrations of iron exceeding 20 mg/l.

Partially blocked tube wells caused many accidents to unwary users of the pumps due to back pressure in the pumps 'jerking' the handles violently. As a result of these conditions casual use was made of untreated surface water that was highly polluted. In some camps it became necessary to supply drinking water by tankers.

2. Sanitation

Many of the refugees were unaccustomed to any form of organised sanitation and indiscriminate defaecation on the ground was extremely common. The main types of sanitation provided were pit latrines and Oxfam aqua privies. The soil in the area was predominantly impervious to water, thus many difficulties were encountered with disposal of sullage water, aqua privy effluent and the liquids in the pit privies. In some camps white ants caused severe damage to wooden structures after a few months use.

3. Organisation

The easiest camps in which to organise good hygenic conditions were those containing not more than 5,000 to 6,000 people. Camps were each provided with a trained sanitary inspector who had a squad of paid refugee/volunteers at his disposal whose duties were:

a. Cleaning pit latrine plates and the area around pit latrines.

b. Keeping wooden pit latrine plates and shelters in good repair.

c. Preparing and maintaining surface drains (ditches) around tube wells to disperse spilled water and around pit latrines to protect them from surface water in the wet season.

d. Digging replacement latrines and making new squatting plates as required.

e. Spraying the huts and latrines periodically with insecticide.

f. Covering and sealing all filled up pit latrines with clean soil.

Many problems are encountered in refugee camps but many sanitary problems can be avoided by careful organisation in the earliest stages. It is important not to consider water supply, and especially sanitation, as afterthoughts. Camps should have sanitation organised first, and where replacement latrines are likely to be needed, space must be allowed for them. Latrines must be sited close to huts, on sloping ground but not so steep as to discourage users who may not be physically fit. Latrines must not be sited close to surface water or wells and under no circumstances must full latrines be emptied by cutting holes through the sides of pits (on sloping ground). Latrine plates can be made of wooden planks of the same general design as shown in Fig. 26 but square plates are preferable. Slatted plates should not be used as they encourage fly breeding. Oil or kerosene added periodically to pit latrines effectively reduces fly breeding which can be as serious a source of enteric disease as polluted water.

Sanitation squads are of the greatest importance to ensure ongoing cleanliness and maintenance. They must be provided with tools — spades, saws, hammers, brushes, buckets, spray machines, etc., and also with timber, nails, wire, kerosene and insecticide. Contingency funds must be allocated for this and for payment of a small remuneration to the working refugees. The sanitary inspector must be free to inspect the condition of latrines and wells regularly and to organise and supervise the squads to carry out all necessary maintenance. This is a form of preventive medicine and must take precedence over his other duties. A suitable size of squad for a camp of 5,000 people is from 20 to 30 depending on local conditions. Some maintenance work such as pit digging is arduous in hot humid climates and due allowance must be made for this.

Organised sanitation meets some resistance in some places and assaults on sanitation volunteers may occur. It is absolutely necessary to ensure that the squads can carry out their very important work without personal risk and if possible with the co-operation of other camp inmates.

Appendix

Planning Piped Water and Sanitation in Developing Towns

Although most people in developing areas live in small scattered communities, inevitably some communities gather more people and develop into towns. Many of the water supply and sanitation systems that can safely be used in small rural communities cannot be used in densely populated towns, but there is still a need to improve water and sanitation services in a systematic way. Where finance is available piped systems are often desirable. Pipelines improve availability of water, consumption may rise to 50 l/h/d where public stand-pipes are used, to more than 150 l/h/d where house connections are provided. An increased consumption of water inevitably means increased discharge of waste, and may also exceed the capacity of some water sources. Pipelines have the advantages of protecting water supplies from pollution from the environment, and protecting the environment from pollution by sewage. However, before introducing pipelines, the ability of water sources to sustain the increased demand, and the adequacy of waste water disposal facilities to dispose of all wastes safely at all times, should be established. Local water-using industries must be urged to pay particular attention to these constraints. Changes in traditional systems require that great care and tact is exercised to ensure that the new developments are accepted by the users, and properly used and maintained.

Development planners must obtain detailed local information on the water sources, the users, the local climate, the quantity and quality of waste water, local health problems, resources, and the level of local skills and abilities in order to select and design a system that will integrate with the local conditions. The components of such a system are shown in Fig. 41 where some pathways of flow are inevitable but others must be avoided. Successful planning depends on good diagnosis of local problems, appropriate design, the appraisal of resources, sound construction, good operation and maintenance, continuous evaluation and the anticipation of probable future needs. There must be a clear statement of the objectives which might include — adequate supply of good water for all, safe disposal of waste, protection of public health, protection of the environment, re-use of treated wastes, preservation of amenity and the achievement of low capital and operating costs. Sound design of systems is quantitative, therefore site surveys are necessary especially in unfamiliar areas to collect data on:

1. Population number, density and distribution.

Fig.41 WATER USAGE CYCLE

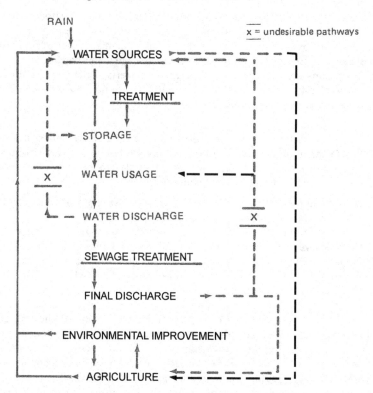

2. Site topography, soil conditions and climate.
3. Existing water source quality availability and quantity used.
4. Existing waste quantity and quality.
5. Health problems prevailing in the community.
6. Existing and potential local industries.
7. Available local resources, land, power, labour, skills, etc.

Water-related local health problems are best considered in groups associated with relevant corrective action. Some public health action such as health education or clinics may be necessary in addition to the water programme.

1. Waterborne diseases — Typhoid, Cholera, Infective Hepatitis, Dysentery, Enteric Diarrhoeas — corrective action, source protection, improved distribution, disinfection.
2. Water-washed diseases — Scabies, Trachoma, Dysentery, — corrective action, increase volume available.

89

3. Water-based diseases — Schistosomiasis, Guinea worm — corrective action, protect source and user.
4. Water-related vector diseases — Malaria, Yellow fever, Onchocerciasis — corrective action, drainage, pipe water from source, anti-vector campaigns.
5. Chemical-based diseases — Methaemoglobinaemia, Fluoridosis, Toxic metal sickness — corrective action, specific appropriate water treatment.
6. Sanitation-based diseases — Hookworm, Ascaris, Trichuris, Leptospirosis and many of those in groups 1 and 2 — corrective action, hygiene education, latrine program, sewage treatment.

Inadequate sanitation is much more common than unsafe water in towns, and is often the major source of pollution and health hazards in water supplies; it may in fact often deserve a higher priority than development of the water supply. Procedure is similar for all sizes of community.

1. Measure number of population, quantity and strength of wastes to be treated, industrial wastes and seasonal run-off.
2. Consider means of waste disposal available, to sea, to permanent rivers, to seasonal rivers, to agriculture.
3. Prepare designs appropriate to local climate and other local requirements.
4. Ensure that operation and maintenance can be sustained.

A critical stage is the onsite examination of the sewage. In tropical areas flow and strength can differ widely from those found in Europe or the US, and designs should use local measurements in preference to those often quoted for European or US communities. Representative samples should be taken on site over several full 24 hour periods together with measurement of flow. Spot samples are not sufficient. Samples should be analysed as quickly as possible, delays enable chemical changes in the samples to render results useless. Special attention must be paid to industrial wastes. When flow-composited estimates of critical parameters are calculated they should be checked against the population numbers and the volume of water used.

The most important analyses required are:

Suspended solids — for design of settlement and sludge disposal.

BOD (5 days at 20°C or 3 days at 27°C) — an essential parameter in the loading rate of secondary treatment systems.

PV or COD — The relation between PV or COD and BOD indicates the biodegradability of wastes.

Ammoniacal N and Phosphate P — essential nutrients in biodegradation. Should be present in proportion to BOD not less than BOD/N/P = 100/5/1.

pH — The favourable range for secondary treatment processes is from about 6.0 to 8.5.

Other analyses such as temperature, DO, H_2S and toxic substances may also be required.

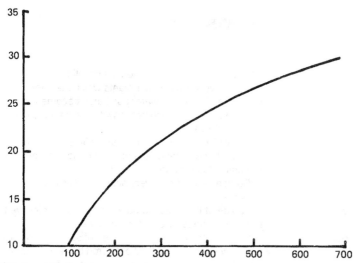

Temperature °C.
Mean of coldest month

BOD Load Kg/ha/day

Fig. 42 Relationship of temperature and area loading rate, for stabilization ponds, 1.25-1.75 m deep, Kg/ha/d of BOD.

BOD tests are particularly necessary in the design of stabilization pond systems. The relationship between temperature and BOD loading per unit surface area is shown in Fig. 42.

Treatment processes for drinking water must also be designed quantitatively using chemical analysis of representative samples of raw water. Variations caused by flood or other local conditions must be considered. Although the major objective should be the provision of drinking water that complies with the minimum WHO quality standards, it is possible that slightly differing standards, might have to be accepted in some cases. Where water sources are seasonally dry, provision must be made for storage to ensure supplies in dry periods.

Chemical analysis of samples should include — Colour, Turbidity, Suspended Solids, pH, Alkalinity, Iron, Manganese, Copper and Fluoride. Organic pollution can be measured by Ammonia, Nitrite, Nitrate, PV and Chlorine demand tests. In some cases coagulation tests can be carried out on site to determine coagulant dose and the reaction rates.

Where sewage or raw water are found to have special problems small pilot scale studies can be set up to test the efficiency of corrective processes and allow the design of full-scale facilities to be established on the basis of actual local conditions. It is important to recognize that the same treatment system cannot be expected to function well on the wide variety of water and sewages that may be found, or in the great range of climatic environments that exists.

91

Glossary

Aerobic	– action for which air or oxygen is essential.
Algal growth	– growth of very small water plants which may help to reduce pollution in water but if they become too numerous cause difficulties in water treatment such as clogging filters etc.
Anaerobic	– action which occurs out of contact with air or oxygen.
Bacterial count	– a method of estimating the number of bacteria present per unit volume of water.
Bilharzia	– a disease caused by a very small free swimming parasite.
Bilharzia cercaria	– the stage of the Bilharzia parasite when it is infective to man. Infection is by penetration of the skin.
Colloidal material	– solid particles suspended in water, of such a small size that they cannot be settled or filtered by simple means.
Correlation	– a mathematical relationship
Desludging	– the removal of accumulated sludge from settling tanks, aqua privies, septic tanks, etc. If this is not carried out properly the level of sludge will build up and seriously affect the action of the apparatus and may cause serious nuisance.
Effluent	– any liquid discharge
Empirical	– by trial and error
Excavated	– dug in the soil
Faecal pollution	– pollution or impurity caused by the excreta of animals and humans, may be a source of disease organisms.
Fissured rock	– rock containing many cracks which may behave as water channels
Flocculation and coagulation	– processes in which chemicals are added to water to produce a precipitate which combines with solid material suspended in the water and enables it to settle to the bottom leaving a clear top layer
Frictional headloss	– a loss of pressure in a pipe caused by friction between the flow of liquid and the pipe itself. It is measured as the difference in head level required to overcome the headloss
Friable	– dry and crumbly
Gravity sewers	– sewers utilizing natural drainage without the use of pumps
Humus	– stable organic matter found in soil and necessary for good moisture retention etc.
Hydraulic short-circuiting	– takes place when the inlet and outlet of a tank or pond are

close together and flow takes the shortest possible path allowing a large volume of the liquid to be undisturbed.

Impervious — watertight

Latitude — the angular distance due north or south between any place and the equator which is 0°. The value can be found with sufficient accuracy by consulting a map or atlas.

Limestone — mineral consisting mainly of calcium carbonate ($CaCO_3$). It is not the same as lime, oxide of lime, quicklime or road-lime which are all calcium oxide (CaO) or slaked lime which is calcium hydroxide ($Ca(OH)_2$). These other substances can be used to correct acidity but they are more soluble in water and needed to be dosed in the correct proportions.

Methane gas — an inflammable gas produced by the anaerobic fermentation of organic material such as sludge

Pathogenic organisms — organisms responsible for disease.

Peak demand — highest rate of consumption measured at any time, in practice the peak demand may last for no more than a few minutes. It may be found when all taps and other outlets in a system are operating fully open at the same time.

Permeable strata — layers of soil or other minerals through which water can freely drain. Impermeable strata such as clay will retain water and prevent drainage

Photosynthesis — the behaviour of plants which liberate oxygen by day and carbon dioxide after dark

Polythene film — thin sheet plastic material, preferably black in colour. This material is often used in coffee factories and may be known as coffee sheeting. Thicker material can be obtained and is more durable

Precipitation — a change which enables dissolved substances to separate from solutions as solid particles

Pro rata — in proportion to the rate (of flow)

Quiescent — still or undisturbed

Retention time — time that flowing water is retained in tanks, filters, etc. It may be calculated from the volume of tank and the rate of flow $RT = \dfrac{\text{volume of tank}}{\text{rate of flow}}$

Revetement — lining of wood, stone or any suitable material to prevent the walls of pits or channels collapsing in soft soil

Sand filtration — the process in which solid particles are removed from water by the straining action of beds of sand

Sedimentation *(settlement)* — the process in which solid particles are allowed to fall to the bottom of a body of water in a sedimentation tank or settlement tank

Sieve — a perforated screen usually of wire mesh. There is a British Standard specification for the sizes of the holes in the mesh but as sizes are quoted in inches and mm, any suitable wire mesh or perforated metal sheet with the correct size holes may be used.

Specific surface area — of a percolating filter medium is the sum of the areas of each

93

piece of medium in a unit volume, there is some loss where the pieces touch. The specific surface area must not be confused with the plan or cross sectional area of a filter. The specific surface area of gravel of 5 to 8 cm grade is about 80 m^2/m^3, larger size gravels have a smaller specific surface and larger volumes may be required to provide the same net specific surface area

Sterilization — any process for rendering bacteria and other organisms harmless

Stock solution — a chemical solution of known strength which can be diluted for use

Superstructure — construction above ground i.e. the superstructure of an aqua privy is the shelter and toilet arrangements

Toxic substances — substances that are harmful or poisonous to biological organisms (including those responsible for treatment processes)

Turbidity — muddy or cloudy appearances in water caused by masses of small floating particles

Voids — the spaces between sand grains or gravel

Weir — a barrier in a stream or open water channel over which water must flow. Weirs can be used to measure rates of flow.

94

Further Reading

Sewage treatment

1. "Small sewage treatment works". British Standard Code of Practice CP302, 1972.
2. "Excreta disposal for rural areas and small communities". Wagner, E.G. and Lanoix, J.N. WHO Monograph No. 39, 1958.
3. "Rural sanitation in the tropics". Bulletin No. 8, Ross Institute, London Sc. of Hyg. and Trop. Med.
4. "Composting" — Gotaas, H.B. WHO Monograph No. 31, 1956.
5. "Waste stabilization ponds" — Gloyna, E.G. WHO Monograph No. 60, 1971.
6. "Waste stabilization ponds" — Arcievala, S.J., et al. Central Pub. Health Eng. Research Inst. Nagpur, India, 1970.
7. "Waste treatment lagoons". Water Poll. Con. Res. Series 17090 EXH 07/71 US Environmental Protection Agency.
8. "River pollution". Klein, L. 3 vols. Butterworths, London.
9. "Guide to simple sanitary measures for the control of enteric diseases". S. Rajagopalan, M.A. Shiffman, WHO 1974.

Water supply

1. "Water supply for rural areas and small communities". Wagner, E.G. and Lanoix, J.N. WHO Monograph No. 42, 1959.
2. "Principles of water quality control" — Tebbutt, T.H.Y. Commonwealth and International Library of Science Technology Engineering and Liberal Studies — Pergamon Press, 1971.
3. "Operation and control of water treatment processes". Cox, C.R. WHO Monograph No. 48, 1964.
4. "Military engineering Vol. VI. Water supply" 1936, HMSO.
5. "Rural water supply and sanitation". Wright, F.B. John Wiley & Sons Chapman & Hall, 1939.
6. "The examination of waters and water supplies". Windle Taylor, E. 8th ed. Churchill, London, 1958. Earlier editions are also very useful.
7. "Methods of testing water used in industry". BS 2690/1956.

8. "Water and waste water engineering". Fair, G.H., Geyer, J.G. and Okun, D.A
9. "Manual of British Water Supply Practice". Institution of Water Engineers London.
10. "More Water for Arid Lands" National Academy of Sciences, Washington DC 1974.
•11. "Drawers of Water", G.F. White, D.J. Bradley, A.U. White. Chicago University Press.
12. "Rural Water supply and Sanitation in Less Developed Countries" A.U. White C. Seviour IDRC-02SC 1974.

Further Information

Further information and advice on small-scale water treatment and sanitation systems may be obtained by writing to the following organisations. There are many others who may be able to help. The same organisations would be most interested in receiving reports from those who have designed, built, or operated any of the devices described, or any other simple systems.

Information of this kind can be extremely useful in indicating the areas in which research should be concentrated, and in revealing problems for which the solutions are not yet readily available.

Intermediate Technology Development Group Ltd.
103-105 Southampton Row, London WC1B 4HH.

Water Research Centre, (For the attention of H. Mann)
Elder Way, Stevenage, Herts. England.

London School of Hygiene and Tropical Medicine, Keppel Street, Gower Street
.London WC1, England.

World Health Organisation,
Reference Centre for Community Water Supplies
13 Parkweg, The Hague. Netherlands.

Other ITDG Publications on water and sanitation

1. A Manual on the Automatic Hydraulic Ram Pump by Simon Watt. 1975.
2. Chinese Chain and Washer Pumps compiled by Simon Watt. 1976.
3. Hand Dug Wells and Their Construction by S. Watt and W.E. Wood. 1977.
4. Hand Pump Maintenance in the Context of Community Well Projects compiled by Arnold Pacey. 1977.
5. Ferrocement Water Tanks and Their Construction by S.B. Watt. 1978.
6. Small Scale Irrigation by Peter Stern. 1979.

For full publications list with details of prices write to Intermediate Technology Publications, 103-105 Southampton Row, London WC1B 4HH.

96

CPSIA information can be obtained
at www.ICGtesting.com
Printed in the USA
JSHW020811041022
31262JS00006B/140